Philadelphia, Pa. Messiah's Church

Hymns, Principles of Faith, Church Order

and divine services or occasional liturgy, for the use of Messiah's church

Philadelphia, Pa. Messiah's Church

Hymns, Principles of Faith, Church Order
and divine services or occasional liturgy, for the use of Messiah's church

ISBN/EAN: 9783337780647

Printed in Europe, USA, Canada, Australia, Japan

Cover: Foto ©Lupo / pixelio.de

More available books at **www.hansebooks.com**

Principles of Faith,

CHURCH ORDER,

AND

DIVINE SERVICES,

OR

OCCASIONAL LITURGY;

FOR THE USE OF

MESSIAH'S CHURCH.

"I will sing with the spirit, and I will sing with the understanding also. I will pray with the spirit, and I will pray with the understanding also." 1 Cor. xiv. 15.

PHILADELPHIA:
PUBLISHED BY J. LITCH,
127 NORTH 11TH STREET.
1860.

INTRODUCTION.

"MESSIAH'S CHURCH," as a distinctive name, has been adopted as expressive of our faith in Jesus of Nazareth, as the Messiah *in the Hebrew sense of that word*, a personal, visible king, of David's line, to reign in Jerusalem, in the resurrection state, and in the renewed earth, in fulfilment of the promise made by Gabriel to MARY before His birth. "Thou shalt call his name Jesus. He shall be great, and shall be called the Son of the Highest. And the Lord God shall give unto Him the throne of His father David, and He shall reign over the house of Jacob forever, and of His kingdom there shall be no end." Luke i. 31, 32. All of which we receive in its literal acceptation. A Messiah who shall not fulfil this promise is not our Messiah, nor the Messiah of Scripture. We take this name, to give prominence to this much-neglected and rejected truth. All Christians profess faith in the second advent of Christ; but differ on the object and manner of that advent. We believe it will be personal and visible, to judge the world, restore paradise, and reign. We have embodied our views of the leading doctrines of Scripture, and Scriptural forms of government, that we may the better "All speak the same thing and be joined together in one mind," and that we may give united and distinct testimony of our faith on points on which we are agreed. We do this, not in the character of legislators, but of students of the Word, disciples of Christ, embodying what we trust we have learned from His Word of the mind of the great Lawgiver on these points; while to that great constitution, the charter of our rights and duties, we appeal on all questions; and to its mandates we humbly bow. Whatever we there find, we will believe and practise.

Our object is, to be ourselves prepared, and to assist in preparing a people for the speedy coming of our blessed Lord, by holding up before our own minds and the minds of others this great sanctifying truth. The attainment of the highest standard of Christian holiness, and the conversion and salvation of the greatest number of sinners, is the object of our highest ambition.

We have appended "DIVINE SERVICES," for

various occasions, as a guide to those who otherwise might feel embarrassed in engaging in those services, and that all things may be done decently and in order.

We have supplied a small collection of choice Hymns to aid our devotions. We trust they will not be unacceptable to the church.

J. Litch,
D. Campbell,
J. T. Laning,
Wm. Prideaux,
} *Committee of Publication.*

Philadelphia, March 1st, 1860.

Principles of Divine Truth,

BELIEVED AND MAINTAINED BY MESSIAH'S CHURCH.

THE HOLY SCRIPTURES.

The Holy Scriptures are a Divine revelation of the person, character, works, purposes, promises, threatenings, and laws of God, in His dealings and intercourse with this world; that is, this globe and its inhabitants. Holy men wrote them as they were moved by the Holy Spirit. In them God has spoken as He means, and means as He says. His word, therefore, is to be interpreted by the same laws of language by which all other writings are interpreted— the meaning of each part to be determined by the subject and the context, in the light of parallel passages. And yet, so profound are these Divine writings, that it is only by the assistance and illumination of the Holy Spirit that their full import and richness can be apprehended. It is a great and dangerous error, to teach that the Bible is a mystical book, and does not express its meaning in plain terms, but leaves it to the fancy of each interpreter to put on it his own construction; thus striking at the foundation of all confidence in it as an infallible standard of truth and rule of faith, and leaving us precisely where we should be without the Bible. But, interpreting it by the ordinary laws of language, the Bible is a sufficient and perfect rule of faith and duty.

OF GOD.

There is but ONE living and true God, who is a Spirit, eternal, omnipresent, omniscient, of infinite wisdom, power, goodness, truth, justice, and mercy. He is the Creator and Ruler of all things visible and invisible. In Him we all live, and move, and have our being. He is manifested to us by the Scriptures as Father, Word, and Holy Spirit.

OF JESUS CHRIST.

Jesus of Nazareth is the Christ, the king of Israel, the Saviour of the world. He was begotten of the Holy Spirit, born of Mary, a pure virgin, and was therefore the only begotten Son of God, the Son of man, and the seed of the woman. In this man, Jesus the Christ, dwelt all the fulness of the Godhead bodily, the Word which was in the beginning with God, and was God; hence, he was both God and man. He bore our sins in His own body on the tree, and by His death became the propitiation for our sins, and not for ours only, but also for the sins of the whole world, so that God can be just, and yet the justifier of him that believeth in Jesus. He rose from the dead, the first fruits of them that slept, and was declared to be the Son of God, with power according to the Spirit of holiness by the resurrection from the dead. After being seen of his disciples forty days, He ascended to heaven, visibly and bodily, and sat down on the right hand of God. To them that look for Him shall He appear the second time, without sin, unto salvation, and will come in like manner as His disciples saw Him go into heaven.

OF THE HOLY GHOST.

The Holy Ghost has been sent into the world by the Father, through the mediation of the Son, as the inspirer of truth, the reprover of sin, the awakener of the conscience, the renewer, sanctifier, and comforter of the penitent and obedient believer, the witness of adoption, the seal and earnest of the saint's inheritance; He dwells in each child of God, and will, at the glorious appearing of Jesus Christ, quicken the mortal bodies of the saints into immortal life, and will dwell in them eternally, constituting them the children of God.

OF MAN.

God made man holy and immortal, composed of a body, made of dust; a soul, the life or living principle, produced by the Divine being when he breathed into man's nostrils the breath of life; and a spirit, the conscious principle, formed within him. Mortality or death is the fruit of sin, the penalty of the law of God. It consists in a disseverance of the spiritual and physical nature of man, so that the dust returns to the earth as it was, and the spirit to God who gave it. In this intermediate state, between death and the resurrection, the righteous enter into peace, and are comforted; but the wicked in hades, that is, the invisible world, are tormented. But the righteous do not receive their crowns nor inheritance till after the general judgment, the second advent of Christ, and the resurrection of their bodies; nor do the wicked receive their punishment till the same epoch.

OF THE FALL.

God created and made this world in perfection, for man's dominion and inheritance, and made man holy and immortal, to enjoy and rule it. The first act of disobedience, by our first parents, brought death on the race, and the curse on the world; so that man is sinful and mortal, and the whole creation groaneth and travaileth in pain together until now, waiting for the manifestation of the sons of God; while the usurper, Satan, claims the right of possession and dominion over all the kingdoms of the world.

OF SALVATION.

Salvation is pardon, restoring the guilty to the favour of God; renewal and sanctification, restoring the depraved and polluted to moral purity and holiness; glorification, restoring the mortal and corruptible from the ruins of the fall to immortality and glory. It embraces, also, a deliverance of man's inheritance from the curse and the dominion of Satan, and man's restitution to its everlasting enjoyment. Then, not before, will salvation be complete.

OF CONDITIONS OF SALVATION.

The conditions of pardon and sanctification are, repentance toward God, and faith in our Lord Jesus Christ. The condition of eternal salvation to the believer is, continuous faith in and obedience to Christ, to the end.

OF THE RESURRECTION OF THE DEAD.

There will be a resurrection of the bodies of all the race of Adam who die, both of the just and the unjust. The just will be raised to everlasting life at the second coming of Christ, and the introduction of the millennium. The unjust will be raised at the end of the millennium, when Satan is loosed from his prison; and, under his deceptive influence, they will go up from the four quarters of the earth to assault and attempt to overthrow Christ and His saints in the New Jerusalem; then fire from God, out of heaven, will come down and devour them, and whoever is not found written in the book of life, will be cast into the lake of fire, which is the second death; the joys of the righteous, and sufferings of the wicked, will then be eternal. The only millennium taught in the Bible, is between the resurrection of the just and the unjust, and consists in Christ's personal reign with his saints, for a thousand years, the Sabbath of Creation.

OF THE CONVERSION OF THE WORLD.—THE JEWS.

The Scriptures do not teach the conversion of the greater part of our race, or the return of the Jews as a nation to their own land, at any period previous to the coming of the Messiah. The theories which have been advocated on these points were unknown to the primitive church.

OF THE KINGDOM OF GOD.

The kingdom of God is the glorious and everlasting reign of Christ on the throne of David in the New Jerusalem, the metropolis of the new earth, with His redeemed and glorified people; thus fulfilling Revelation xi. 15: "The kingdoms of this world are become the kingdoms of our Lord and His Christ; and He shall reign forever and ever."

OF THE EVERLASTING ABODE OF THE SAINTS.

The Scriptures speak thus, in reference to the everlasting abode of the saints in a glorified state. Isaiah lxv. 17: "For behold, I create new heavens and a new earth; and the former shall not be remembered nor come into mind." Isa. lxv. 17: "But be ye glad and rejoice for ever in that which I create." Matt. v. 5:

"Blessed are the meek, for they shall inherit the earth." 2 Pet. iii. 13: "Nevertheless we, according to His promise, look for new heavens and a new earth, wherein dwelleth righteousness." Daniel vii. 27: "And the kingdom and dominion, and the greatness of the kingdom under the whole heaven, shall be given to the people of the saints of the Most High, whose kingdom is an everlasting kingdom, and all dominions shall serve and obey Him." Rev. v. 10: "And hast made us unto our God kings and priests; and we shall reign on the earth." Rev. xx. 6: "Blessed and holy is he that hath part in the first resurrection, on such the second death hath no power, but they shall be priests of God and of Christ, and shall reign with Him a thousand years." Rev. xxi. 1, 3, 4: "And I saw a new heaven and a new earth, for the first heaven and the first earth had passed away; and there was no more sea. And I heard a great voice out of heaven, saying, Behold the tabernacle of God is with men, and He shall dwell with them, and they shall be His people, and God himself shall be with them, and be their God. And God shall wipe away all tears from their eyes; and there shall be no more death, neither sorrow nor crying, neither shall there be any more pain; for the former things are passed away."

OF THE TIME OF THE ADVENT.

Though we do not fix the definite time when the Son of Man shall come in His glory, yet the fulfilment of the prophecies and the events in the history of the church and the world, which have taken place, and are now transpiring, give evidence that He is nigh, even at the door. It is the duty of Christians to watch and pray always, that they may be accounted worthy to escape all those things that shall come to pass, and to stand before the Son of Man. The second advent of Christ, and the truths connected with that great event, are to be taught in connexion with the various truths belonging to the gospel of Christ, as they present Scriptural motives for awakening and sanctifying the children of men.

OF CONVERSION.

Men are converted to God through truth as an instrument, applied to their souls by the power of the Holy Spirit. Without this change, they are dead in trespasses and sins. Of His own will begat he us with the word of truth, that we should be a kind of first-fruits of His creatures.

OF DUTIES OF CHRISTIANS.

Believers should love God and their fellow-men, being careful to maintain good works. They are to place their affections on things above, not on things on the earth. It is their duty to continue instant in prayer—to pray with and instruct their families in the truth of God; to be watchful. They are not to be conformed to the world; but to follow the example of Christ, in meekness, forbearance, kindness, and love to the souls of men, constantly imploring the influence of the Holy Spirit, studying the Scriptures, that they may honour and obey their Master's will, and be made free by the truth. As they have opportunity, they are to do good to all men. especially to them that are of the household of faith. In short, they are to live soberly, righteously and godly in this present world, looking for that blessed hope, and the glorious appearing of the great God, even our Saviour Jesus Christ.

OF A VISIBLE CHURCH.

A church organized according to the New Testament, is composed of persons, who give evidence that they believe in Christ, and show their faith by their works, and who observe the ordinances according to the direction of the Scriptures. Each church has power to receive members, to watch over them, to admonish them, to dismiss them, or to put them away for violations of the rules of the Gospel.

OF THE DUTY OF CONFESSING CHRIST.

Those who are converted to Christ should confess His name before men, and, according to His command and example, should be baptized in His name.

OF THE LORD'S SUPPER.

The Lord's Supper is to be observed by the church in its collective capacity, that His death may be shown till He come.

BASIS OF CHURCH FELLOWSHIP.

We, followers of the Lord Jesus Christ, who are looking for His speedy personal advent to reign on earth, believing the Scriptures of the Old and New Testaments to be a revelation from God, and a perfect rule of faith and practice, do covenant with God and each other to be governed by that rule; to meet together, and exhort one another, and so much the more as we see the day approaching. We promise faithfulness to each other in submitting to and enforcing gospel discipline. And as we believe that Christ has but one church on earth, and that it is composed of all truly penitent and obedient believers in him, we receive as our brethren, all such as by a godly walk and love for His appearing, evince those characteristics.

CHURCH ORDER.

THE MINISTRY.

The recognised ministry of the church as taught in the New Testament, consists of Bishops or Elders, Evangelists, Pastors, and Teachers, whose functions are to be performed by individuals as the Spirit may dispense to each His gifts, calling and qualifying them for their work, and as they shall be recognised by the church. Eph. iv. 11—13; Titus i. 5—9; 1 Tim. v. 17—19.

In addition to the foregoing, persons giving promise of gifts should be encouraged to exercise and make manifest those gifts by letters of commendation or license.

OFFICERS OF THE CHURCH.

1. A Secretary, to keep all records of the church.

2. A Board of Trustees, where real estate is to be held.

3. Ruling Elders or Deacons,* to assist the ministers in the government of the church, and especially to take charge of its finances, provide for the support of the pastor, and sick and aged poor. They shall be constituted by the voice of the church, and after prayer, by laying on of hands and blessing of the ministry. Their term of service shall expire at the end of one year; but after three elections by the church, their office shall be permanent, during good behaviour. The ordination shall not be repeated when re-elected. 1 Tim. iii. 8—13; Acts vi. 1—6.

SUPPLY OF THE DESK AND CALL OF A PASTOR.

The Ruling Elders or Deacons shall provide temporary supplies for the Desk. But the call and settlement of a pastor shall be by the voice of the church, in a meeting publicly called for that purpose. In case of circuits, the call shall be by the voice of the Quarterly Conference. Those preferring an itinerant ministry, may arrange with the Messianian Missionary Society for such supply.

* Churches can have either Ruling Elders or Deacons, or both, as they deem expedient.

SUPPORT OF THE MINISTRY.

The Lord has ordained that they who preach the gospel should live of the gospel. In order to succeed in raising funds, let there be a system adopted. 1 Cor. ix. chap.

1. The Deacons should inform the church at the beginning of each year of the estimated expenses for the year.

2. The church should direct what course shall be adopted to raise the amount; whether by subscription or apportionment among the members, or by tithes and offerings.

3. Whatever course is adopted, let the accounts all be closed at the end of each quarter. The quarterly conference should scrupulously attend to this point.

PUBLIC WORSHIP.

Public worship shall, as far as possible, be regularly maintained in every church. 1st. By preaching, or 2d, when that cannot be done, by reading the word, exhortation, singing, and prayer, or by selecting and reading a suitable discourse.

Order of exercises. Singing, reading the Scripture, prayer, singing, sermon, prayer, singing, benediction.

RECEPTION OF MEMBERS.

Any person wishing to unite with the church should make known their wish to a minister or officer of the church, which application should be brought before the church or the official board; and if approved, on the first suitable occasion, if no objection is raised, they should be publicly received.

DUTIES OF MEMBERS.

1. It is expected of all in fellowship with us that they shall abstain from all those acts which would exclude them from the kingdom of heaven, as set forth in the Word of God. Gal. v. 19—21.

2. That they shall be diligent in the performance of all Christian duties, such as reading the word daily, secret and family prayer, a godly example before the world, such as shall glorify God. Gal. v. 22—26.

3. Each member is expected, as far as practicable, to attend and participate in the weekly prayer and conference meeting, which shall be held in such locality and at such time as best to suit the convenience of members. Heb. x. 23—25.

4. To contribute regularly to the support of the gospel, according to their ability, and for the support of the sick and aged poor.

5. On removal, each member should obtain from the minister, or an officer of the church in the minister's absence, a certificate of standing or dismission.

6. If any members habitually absent themselves from the means of grace without reasonable excuse, it shall be the duty of the minister or deacons to visit and labour with them, and endeavour to reclaim them to duty. If after

faithful labour, they shall still persist in neglect, they shall be subject to exclusion from the church for such neglect. Heb. xii. 12—17.

DISCIPLINE.

1. In any case when a brother has trespassed against another, the rule given by Christ, Matth. xviii. 15—17, shall be strictly observed.

2. In case of public transgression and immorality, such as profanity, drunkenness, sorcery, covetousness, &c., the church should inquire into the alleged offence, and if the charge is well founded, and the offender does not give evidence of repentance by confession and reparation, he should be put away after due investigation, that he may not prove a stumbling-block to the world and grief to the church.

3. If complaint is made of injustice, such complainant shall have right of appeal to a council of the official board of the nearest church of our order, or in case of a circuit, to the quarterly conference of the circuit, except such as absent themselves from trial before the church.

CARE OF CHILDREN AND YOUTH.

1. Let all parents and ministers take a special interest in the moral and religious training of the youth of our congregations, and encourage the daily study of God's word.

2. Wherever a few children can be collected, let a Sabbath-school and Bible class be established and provided with believing teachers.

3. The superintendent of such school shall be a member of the quarterly conference, and report when required the state and wants of the school.

4. Each church should report the state of the Sabbath-school to the Annual Conference.

MONTHLY MEETING OF THE CHURCH.

There shall be a monthly meeting of the church for general Christian conference, experience, prayer, and business.

QUARTERLY CONFERENCE.

There shall be held a quarterly Conference of all the official members of the church or pastoral charge, consisting of the Pastor, Licensed and ordained Ministers, Exhorters, Ruling Elders, Deacons, Trustees, Secretary of the church and Sabbath-School Superintendents, for the purpose of mutual conference on the interests of the Church; to license such persons as they, after due examination and inquiry, think proper to preach the gospel, and officiate as exhorters; and to examine into the character and qualifications of candidates for ordination, and decide whether they shall be recommended for ordination to the work of the ministry. Also to discuss and decide such other subjects as may be deemed of importance to the general interests of the church. Special meetings of the Quarterly Conference may be called by the Pastor, or any two members of said conference.

QUESTIONS FOR QUARTERLY CONFERENCE.

1. What is the state of the church or churches?
2. Are the means of grace faithfully attended?
3. Is the Sabbath-School cause sustained?
4. Has the support of the Pastor been raised?
5. What has been done for missions and tracts?
6. Are there any appeals to be considered?
7. Are there any licenses to be granted?
8. Are there any to be recommended for ordination?

ANNUAL CONFERENCES.

There shall be an Annual Conference held in such locality as to accommodate the churches who may be embraced in it; to be composed of one delegate from each church, with all Pastors and ordained ministers, Evangelists and Missionaries, within the bounds of the conference. The conference shall examine into the moral and ministerial character of each ordained minister; elect for ordination such Licentiates as are recommended by the several quarterly conferences, if, in their judgment, after due examination, they are suitable persons; try charges of immoral or disorderly conduct made against ordained ministers; take a general oversight of the Sabbath-School, Bible, Tract, and Missionary cause; hear reports from the churches, and consider such other subjects as may relate to the general interest of the churches, and shall appoint a committee to prepare a course of study for young ministers, and to examine them on those studies.

ORDER OF BUSINESS FOR ANNUAL CONFERENCES.

Each annual conference shall elect its own officers, who shall hold over till new ones are elected.

1. Reading the word, singing and prayer at the opening of each session. 2. Appointment of committees. 3. Choice of officers. 4. Reports from churches. 5. Reports from Sabbath Schools. 6. Examination of character of ministers. 7. Election for ordination. 8. Missionary Society's Report. 9. Special business. 10. Time and place of next conference.

MARRIAGE CEREMONY.

Dearly Beloved:—We have here met in the presence of Almighty God and these witnesses, to join together this man and woman in the holy bonds of Wedlock. This is an institution appointed by the Lord in the days of man's innocency, and ought not to be taken in hand hastily and unadvisedly, but prudently and in the fear of God. And we may hope that all who thus come together, being joined not only in hand but also in heart, will secure to themselves great happiness, and have God's blessing resting upon them. Wherefore, I beseech all present, who may know any just cause why this man and woman may not be thus joined, now to speak; or forever hereafter to keep silence.

No objection being made, the Minister shall say to the Man,

Do you, Sir, take this woman to be your lawful and wedded wife, to live together according to God's holy ordinance of Matrimony; and, abstaining from all others, will you cleave only unto her, in sickness and in health, in wealth and adversity, as long as you both shall live? If so, say Yes.

Then shall he say to the Woman,

And do you take this man to be your lawful and wedded husband, to live together according to God's holy ordinance of Matrimony; and, abstaining from all others, will you cleave only unto him, in sickness and in health, in wealth and adversity, as long as you both shall live? If so, say Yes.

[*In cases where it is desired to use a ring, let the Minister now say to the Man,*

What pledge do you give that you will perform these your vows?

The Man shows the ring, and the Minister says to the Woman,

Do you receive this ring in token of the same on your part?

Then the Man (the Minister guiding his hand) shall place the ring on the fourth finger of her left hand.]

Then shall the Minister cause them to take each other by the right hand, and laying his upon theirs, shall say,

Forasmuch as you have thus plighted your faith each to the other, saying that you take each other to be man and wife, I pronounce you man and wife, in the name of the Father, Son, and Holy Spirit. And what God has joined together, let no man put asunder.

Let us Pray.

O Lord God most merciful, Thou hast heard these promises of Thy servant and handmaid to each other: mercifully condescend to unite their hearts and lives by all the grace and true affection of a happy marriage. May their love never know change, or doubt, or decay. Replenish them with Thy Holy Spirit, that they may piously live together according to Thy divine will. May they be blessed in each other, and both in the knowledge of Christ, Thy Son, and may they at last enter Thy blessed Kingdom: through Jesus Christ our Redeemer. *Amen.*

May the LORD lift up His countenance upon you, and give you peace! And may the blessing of Almighty God, Father, Son, and Holy Spirit, be upon you, for evermore. *Amen.*

DEDICATION OF CHILDREN.

We believe that the Sacrifice of Christ avails for children, as well as for adults; and that He who received the little ones who were brought to Him in the days of His public ministry, is still pleased to receive all those who are solemnly presented to Him by prayer in faith. We regard it as the duty of all persons having children committed to their care, early to dedicate them to Christ, by prayer and the blessing of His ministers; believing that such acts of piety will be approved in heaven, and sanctified to the good of the children and those who present them.

This act of Dedication is not to be looked upon as taking the place of Christian Baptism, which is an ordinance designed for such as have repented of their sins and believe in Christ; and which should be promptly attended to by every believer, whether he was dedicated to Christ in childhood or not.

There should be kept in every church, a record of the names of those who, by the hands of the minister, have been dedicated to Christ; and all such children should be regarded as peculiarly under the watchful care of the church. As soon as they are old enough to comprehend the simpler truths of the Bible, they should be formed into classes, and regularly taught by the Pastor or some other one appointed for that service; and their early conversion and union with the church, should be earnestly prayed for and confidently expected.

In case of the death of the natural guardians of such children, they should be taken under the care of the church, who, by its Pastor and Officers, should carefully watch over all their interests, both temporal and spiritual.

The Minister coming into the altar, shall call

upon those who desire to present their children to God to come forward, and when all have taken their places, shall use the following

INVOCATION.

ALMIGHTY GOD, our Heavenly Father, we meekly beseech Thee, in Thy tender mercy, to look upon us, and be present with us and bless us in this solemn ceremony. Graciously regard Thy servants who bring to Thee the little ones committed to their hands, and mercifully accept their offering. Make them duly sensible of the great responsibilities that rest upon them. Give them a holy and lasting sense of their dependence upon Thee for Thy blessing. Make them to see that henceforth they stand in a new relation to Thee and to their children; and do Thou so abundantly add Thy grace that they may not only understand their duty, but may so discharge it that at the last they may, with their children, stand before Thee and render their account with joy: through our Lord Jesus Christ. *Amen.*

Then the Minister may read the following:

The curse of the LORD is in the house of the wicked; but He blesseth the habitation of the just. Train up a child in the way he should go; and when he is old, he will not depart from it.

And Hannah vowed a vow, and said, O LORD of hosts, if Thou wilt indeed look on the affliction of Thine handmaid, and remember me, and not forget Thine handmaid, but wilt give unto Thine handmaid a man-child, then I will give him unto the LORD all the days of his life. And the LORD remembered Hannah, and she bare a son, and called his name Samuel. And when she had weaned him, she brought him to the house of the LORD in Shiloh, and the child was young. And they slew a bullock, and brought the child to Eli. And she said, O my lord, I am the woman that stood by thee here, praying to the LORD. For this child I prayed; and the LORD hath given me the petition which I asked of Him: therefore, also, I have lent him to the LORD; as long as he liveth, he shall be lent to the LORD.

And Jesus took a child and set him in the midst of them: and when he had taken him in his arms, He said unto them: Except ye be converted and become as little children, ye shall not enter into the kingdom of heaven: whosoever, therefore, shall humble himself as this little child, the same is greatest in the kingdom of heaven. Whosoever shall receive one of such children in my name, receiveth me; and whosoever shall receive me, receiveth not me, but him that sent me. And whosoever shall offend one of these little ones that believe in me, it were better for him that a millstone were hanged about his neck, and he were cast into the sea.

And they brought young children unto Him that He should touch them and pray; and His disciples rebuked those that brought them. But when Jesus saw it, He was much displeased, and called them unto Him and said unto them: Suffer the little children to come unto me, and forbid them not; for of such is the kingdom of God. Verily I say unto you, whosoever shall not receive the kingdom of God as a litttle child, he shall not enter therein. And He took them up in His arms, put His hands upon them and blessed them.

Then let the Minister say to those who bring the little children,

DEARLY BELOVED, ye have heard in these words of Holy Writ, how God promises His blessing to the families of such as love Him; how in ancient times little children were dedicated to Him, and how our Lord Jesus Christ blamed those who would have kept them from Him.

How great is God's *mercy*, and how great is the *duty* that now is before you! It is no small mercy for *this child* to be accepted of God, through the blood of our Lord Jesus Christ, and to have vouchsafed unto *him* God's protection and provision, the means and Spirit of grace, and the renewed pardon of sin upon repentance. The duty on your part, is, first, to see that you *yourselves* are partakers of the faith and covenant of Christ, and ever remain steadfast in the same. And then, that you be diligent and careful to nurture and instruct your children in the true knowledge and fear of God; keeping them from the influence of the ungodly; commanding them after you, as did Abraham, that they may keep the way of the LORD; being careful that, through lack of knowledge, they do not turn away from him. And do you see to it most religiously, that they are taught to flee from and abhor all unbelief, superstition and idolatry; and rest for salvation upon the righteousness of Christ alone; praying ever for light and help from on high, that in the great day of Christ's coming, you may, with all your little ones, rejoice to see Him, saying, Behold I and the children whom God hath given me.

Then the Minister shall take the child into his arms; or, if it is of sufficient age, he shall require it to kneel, and say to those who present it,

Name this child.

And then naming it after them, he shall lay his hands upon it, and say,

Receiving thee at the hands of thy guardians, I solemnly dedicate thee to God, and bless thee, in the name of the Father, Son and Holy Spirit. The LORD bless thee and keep thee. The LORD make His face to shine upon thee, and be gracious unto thee. The Lord lift up His countenance upon thee, and give thee peace!

Then shall the Minister say,

Let us Pray.

ALMIGHTY and most merciful God, our Heavenly Father, we thank Thee that Thou dost suffer little children to come unto Thee, and that Thou dost ordain praise out of the mouths of babes and sucklings. Almighty Father, since it hath pleased Thee, of Thine infinite mercy, to promise that Thou wilt be a God unto us and to our children: we pray Thee to confirm this grace unto the *child* now solemnly dedicated to Thy service by the imposition of our hands. And even as *he* is offered and consecrated unto Thee, so wilt Thou receive *him* into Thy holy protection, declaring Thyself to be *his* God and Saviour, forgiving *him* the original sin whereof the whole race of Adam is guilty; and sanctifying *him* by Thy Holy Spirit: that when he shall come to years of discretion, *he* may know and worship Thee as *his* only God, and glorify Thee throughout all *his* life.

And, O Lord, we humbly beseech Thee to abundantly bless those who thus bring their little ones to Thee. Teach them their duty to their children, and enable them to train them up in the way they should go, that when they are old they may not depart from it. And do Thou, O Lord, incline the hearts of the children to fulfil their duties to their parents. Make every child to feel its obligations to keep its father's commandment, and forsake not the law of its mother.

Shepherd of Israel, rebuke the unbelief of Thy Church respecting the conversion of children, even as Thou didst rebuke Thy disciples when they would have hindered such from coming to Thee. Let none despise these little ones; for Thou hast warned us that their angels do always behold the face of their Father in heaven.

Hear us in these our requests, O God, most merciful, and grant us an answer in peace, for the sake of Jesus Christ our Lord; at whose speedy appearing in the clouds of heaven, may all who are thus dedicated to Thee, be found in His glorious likeness, and be partakers of the heavenly inheritance of Thy saints, world without end. *Amen.*

BURIAL SERVICE.

When approaching the grave, and while the body is being committed to the earth, let the minister repeat one or more of the following sentences, as may be convenient.

MAN that is born of a woman, is of few days, and full of trouble. He cometh forth as a flower, and is cut down: he fleeth also as a shadow, and continueth not.

All flesh is grass, and all the goodliness thereof is as the flower of the field. They are like grass which groweth up. In the morning it flourisheth, and groweth up: in the evening it is cut down and withereth.

We brought nothing into this world, and it is certain we can carry nothing out. Naked came I out of my mother's womb, and naked shall I return thither; the LORD gave and the LORD taketh away, blessed be the name of the LORD.

Then shall the minister say,

Forasmuch as it hath pleased Almighty God, in His all-wise providence, to take out of this clayey tabernacle the soul that inhabited it, we therefore commit the decaying remains to their kindred element; earth to earth, dust to dust, ashes to ashes; looking for a resurrection through our Lord Jesus Christ, who will judge the quick and the dead; and by whose power the earth and the sea shall give up the dead which are in them, and every man be rewarded according to the deeds done in the body. Blessed and holy is he that hath part in the first resurrection: on such the second death hath no power, but they shall be priests of God and of Christ, and shall reign with him a thousand years.

If it be deemed expedient that an Address should be delivered, let it be introduced here.

Let us pray.

O blessed God, the Father of mercies and Author of all consolation, we beseech Thee to look down upon us in pity and compassion. It hath pleased Thee to call away another of our fellow mortals, and thus Thou dost again assure us that we too must die. O LORD, regard in tender mercy those who are especially afflicted by this dispensation of Thy providence. Pour into their wounded hearts the consolation of Thy blessed Gospel, and help them ere the hour of their great change shall come to be joined unto Christ, who hath brought immortality and eternal life to light, and who alone can take away the sting of Death.

O merciful God, the Father of our Lord Jesus Christ; in whom whosoever believeth shall live, though he die; we meekly beseech Thee teach us the frailty of life and the certainty of death, and while space is given us may we make our calling and election sure. Raise us, we beg Thee, from the death of sin unto the life of righteousness; that when we depart this life we may rest in Christ; and at the last day be found acceptable in Thy sight, and through Him who only hath immortality have our portion in the new earth, where tears shall be wiped from off all faces, and where there shall be no more death. Grant this, we beseech Thee, O merciful Father, through Jesus Christ, our Mediator and Redeemer. *Amen.*

The grace of our Lord Jesus Christ, and the love of God, and the fellowship of the Holy Ghost, be with us all evermore. *Amen.*

ADMINISTRATION OF BAPTISM.

Lessons to be read from Scripture. Matt. iii. 7—17, or, Acts ii. 37—42, or, Rom. vi. 1—11.

The minister shall then address the person or persons to be baptized as follows:—

DEARLY BELOVED: You have come here to make confession of your faith in Jesus Christ; and that you being baptized into His death, may be also in the likeness of His resurrection, living henceforth a new and spiritual life, by the indwelling of His Holy Spirit, and may thus be assured of salvation with His people, as He has promised those who believe and are baptized. These, on His part, God will most surely bestow, for the sake of His Son, our Lord Jesus Christ; wherefore, it is my duty in the presence of God, and before this congregation, to demand of you that you do make that confession of unfeigned faith, out of a pure conscience, which Almighty God shall accept and answer, by vouchsafing His holy baptism. I demand, therefore,

Do you believe that man is of his own nature corrupt and evil, and is guilty before God, and obnoxious to His judgments? And do you earnestly desire to be delivered from this guilt?

Ans. Such is my faith, and such is my desire.

Are you persuaded of the mercy of God through Jesus Christ, that He willeth not that any should perish, but hath sent His Son to redeem the world; that Jesus Christ hath died for our sins, the just for the unjust; and that He hath ordained this ordinance of baptism as sign of our renunciation of, and death to sin, and faith in, and union with, Christ by His Holy Spirit?

Ans. All this I believe.

Do you renounce and abhor the devil, and all his works, and all evil spirits; the world, and all its glory and vanities, and all sinful desires of the flesh; so that you will not follow nor be led by them?

Ans. I renounce and abhor them all.

Do you believe in God the Father Almighty, maker of heaven and earth?

And in Jesus Christ, His only begotten Son, our Lord? And that He was conceived by the Holy Ghost; born of the Virgin Mary; that He suffered under Pontius Pilate, was crucified, dead, and buried; that He went down into Hades, and also did rise again the third day; that He ascended into heaven, and sitteth at the right hand of God the Father Almighty; and from thence shall come again to judge the quick and dead?

And do you believe in the Holy Ghost; the holy Catholic Church; the communion of saints; the remission of sins; the resurrection of the body, and the life everlasting?

Ans. All this I steadfastly believe.

Wilt thou be baptized in this faith?

Ans. This is my desire.

Do you unfeignedly submit yourself wholly to the will of Christ, and will you obediently keep

God's holy will and commandments, and walk in the same all the days of your life?

Ans. I do submit myself, and will obey.

Let us pray.

Almighty and everlasting God, who, of thy great mercy, didst save Noah and his family in the ark from perishing by water, and also didst lead the children of Israel, Thy people, through the Red Sea, under the cloud, figuring thereby Thy holy baptism; and by the baptism of Thy well-beloved Son Jesus Christ, in the river Jordan, didst leave us an example; We beseech Thee for Thine infinite compassion, mercifully look upon Thy *servant* before Thee, now to be baptized, and grant unto *him* that he may be washed from all *his* sins; and that being delivered from Thy wrath, and sanctified by Thy Spirit, *he* may evermore abide in Thy mystical body; and being steadfast in faith, joyful in hope, and rooted in charity, *he* may so pass the waves of this troublesome world, that *he* may come at last to the land of everlasting life, there to reign with Thee in that new earth wherein dwelleth righteousness, world without end, through Jesus Christ our Lord. *Amen.*

Grant, O Most Merciful God, that the Old Adam in thy *servant* may be so buried, that the new man may be raised up in *him*. Grant that all carnal affections may die in *him*, and that all things belonging to the spirit may live and grow in *him*. Grant that *he* may have power and strength to have victory, and triumph against the Devil, the World, and the Flesh. Wilt Thou at this time detect and expel all the power and wickedness of Satan from body, soul, and spirit, and deliver him from that wicked enemy, and forever preserve him from his invasions; and do Thou cleanse and sanctify *him* in *his* inward being; clothe *him* with the garment of salvation: and thus preparing him for Thy sacred presence, take up Thy abode in *him* forever, for the sake of Jesus Christ. *Amen.*

The minister shall then baptize him, saying, In obedience to the command of the great head of the church, I baptize you, my *Brother*, (or sister) into the name of the Father, and of the Son, and of the Holy Ghost. *Amen.*

Then laying his hands on the head of the baptized, he shall say,—We receive you into the congregation of Christ's flock, and do bless you in the name of the Father, and of the Son, and of the Holy Spirit. And be thou blest and kept unto everlasting life. *Amen.*

The grace of our Lord Jesus Christ, the love of God, our heavenly Father, and the fellowship of the Holy Ghost, rest upon and abide with you forever. *Amen.*

CELEBRATION OF THE LORD'S SUPPER.

The reading of the Scriptures appropriate for the occasion.

THE CONFESSION.

Almighty God, our Heavenly Father, who admittest Thy people unto such wonderful communion, that, partaking by a Divine mystery of the body and blood of Thy dear Son, they should dwell in Him and He in them; We unworthy sinners, approaching to Thy presence, and beholding Thy Divine glory, do abhor ourselves, and repent in dust and ashes. We have sinned, we have sinned, we have grievously sinned against Thee, in thought, in word, and in deed, provoking most justly Thy wrath and indignation against us. We have broken our past vows; we have dishonoured Thy holy name, and profaned Thy holy sanctuary.

Yet now, most merciful Father, have mercy upon us; for the sake of Jesus Christ, forgive us all our sins; deliver us by the inspiration of Thy Holy Spirit, from all uncleanness, in spirit and in flesh; and give unto us heartily to forgive others as we beseech Thee to forgive us, and to serve Thee henceforth in newness of life, to the glory of Thy holy Name, through Jesus Christ, our Lord. *Amen.*

Thus saith the Lord:

If we confess our sins, He is faithful and just to forgive us our sins, and to cleanse us from all unrighteousness.

Whosoever shall call on the name of the Lord shall be saved.

Almighty God, who by the blood of Thy dear Son, hast consecrated unto us a new and living way into the holiest of all; grant unto us, we beseech Thee, the assurance of Thy mercy, and sanctify us by Thy heavenly grace; that we, approaching unto Thee with pure heart and undefiled conscience, may offer unto Thee an offering in righteousness, and duly celebrate these holy mysteries, to the glory of Thy name, through Jesus Christ our Lord. *Amen.*

THE APOSTLES' CREED—*The people following.*

I believe in God the Father Almighty, Maker of Heaven and Earth;

And in Jesus Christ, His only Son our Lord, Who was conceived by the Holy Ghost, Born of the Virgin Mary, Suffered under Pontius Pilate, Was crucified, dead and buried, He descended into Hades; The third day He rose again from the dead; He ascended into Heaven, And sitteth on the right hand of God the Father Almighty;

From thence He shall come to judge the quick and the dead.

I believe in the Holy Ghost; The Holy Catholic Church; the Communion of Saints; The Forgiveness of Sins; The Resurrection of the Body, And the Life Everlasting. *Amen.*

To be read while the offerings for the poor are being made.

Honour the Lord with thy substance, and with the first fruits of all thine increase: so shall thy barns be filled with plenty, and thy presses shall burst out with new wine.

Bring ye all the tithes into the storehouse, and prove me now herewith, and see if I will not open to you the windows of heaven, saith the Lord of Hosts, and pour you out a blessing, that there shall not be room to receive it.

To do good and distribute, forget not; for with such sacrifices God is well pleased.

PRAYER AND THANKSGIVING.

Almighty and most merciful Father, we are unworthy to offer unto Thee any sacrifice; yet, we beseech Thee, accept this our duty and service, who desire to honour Thee, to worship and adore Thy Majesty, and to acknowledge Thee to be our God, and ourselves Thy servants, as we are most bound. And here we do present to Thee ourselves, our souls, and bodies; and dedicate ourselves unto Thy service, renewing our vows, engaging henceforth to obey Thy commandments, to seek Thy will, and to do the things that please Thee.

O God, Thou knowest our frailty; have mercy upon us, and fulfil our vows in us. Send down Thy Holy Spirit upon us, and let the flesh, and all its affections and lusts, be destroyed in us, as by a consuming fire; that we may henceforth yield ourselves to Thee a living sacrifice, holy and acceptable, which is our reasonable service. Hear us Heavenly Father, for the sake of Jesus Christ, Thy Son, to whom with Thee, and the Holy Ghost, one God, be all honour and glory, world without end. *Amen.*

It is meet, right, and our bounden duty, that we should at all times, and in all places, give thanks unto Thee O Lord, Father Almighty, Eternal God, who together with Thine only begotten Son and the Holy Ghost, art One God, and One Lord.

For Thou didst create all things: Thou gavest unto us life and being. Thy providence has provided for and preserved us. By Thy blessing, we and all things living are nourished; and Thou hast replenished us with Thy goodness.

For all Thy bounties, we give Thee thanks.

But, chiefly, that Thou hast ransomed us from death eternal, and given us the joyful hope of everlasting life, through Jesus Christ, Our Lord.

We bless Thee for His incarnation; for His life on earth; for His precious sufferings and death upon the cross; for His resurrection from the dead; and for His glorious ascension to Thy right hand.

We bless Thee for giving the Holy Ghost; for all the ordinances of Thy church; for the communion of all saints in these holy mysteries which we now celebrate. We bless Thee for the hope of everlasting life, and of the glory which shall be brought unto us at the coming and in the kingdom of Thy dear Son.

Thee, Mighty God, Heavenly King, we magnify and praise. We worship and adore Thy glorious name, the name of the Father, and of the Son, and of the Holy Ghost, joining with all the heavenly hosts before Thy throne, and singing unto Thee,

Holy, Holy, Holy, Lord God of Sabaoth; heaven and earth are full of Thy glory. Hosanna in the highest.

THE LORD'S PRAYER.

Our Father, which art in heaven, &c.

The consecration of the bread and wine.

Look upon us, O Lord, and bless and sanctify this bread and this cup.

In the name of the Father, and of the Son, and of the Holy Ghost, we bless this bread and this cup; and beseech Thee, heavenly Father, to send down Thy Holy Spirit, and make them unto us the body and blood of Thy Son Jesus Christ, who in the same night in which he was betrayed, took bread, [here take the bread] and after He had given thanks, He brake it, [here break the bread] and said, Take, eat, this is my body, which is broken for you; this do in remembrance of me.

In like manner, He also took the cup, [here take the cup in hand] after He had supped, saying, This cup is the New Testament in my blood; this do ye, as often as ye do it, in remembrance of me. *Amen.*

We do not presume to come to this Thy table, O Lord, trusting in our own righteousness, but in Thy manifold and great mercies. We are not worthy to so much as to gather up the crumbs under Thy table; but Thou art the same Lord whose property it is always to have mercy. Grant unto us, therefore, gracious Lord, so to eat the flesh of Thy dear Son, and to drink His blood, that our sinful bodies may be made clean by His body, and our souls washed through His most precious blood, that we may ever more dwell in Him and He in us; and that we may receive of Thy mercy, health, both of soul and body, in the communion of the mystical body of Thy Christ. *Amen.*

The celebrant, with the other ministers, elders, and deacons present, shall first receive the bread and wine, and then deliver it to the people. In delivering the bread, it shall be said, THE BODY OF OUR LORD JESUS CHRIST, GIVEN FOR THEE. *In delivering the cup, it shall be said,* THE BLOOD OF OUR LORD JESUS CHRIST, SHED FOR THEE.

The service shall close with a suitable hymn. If straitened for time, the celebrant may omit such parts of the services as he thinks proper, except the prayer and thanksgiving, and consecration.

ORDINATION OF RULING ELDERS AND DEACONS.

Whenever the church shall have duly elected any person or persons to the office of ruling Elder or Deacon, at a suitable time they shall be set before the minister of the congregation for ordination to the office. Their names having been read aloud, the minister shall say to the people:—

Brethren, if any of you know any crime or impediment in any of these persons presented to be ordained Elders or Deacons, for which he ought not to be admitted to that office, let him now make it known.

[If objection is made, the minister shall cease till the accused be found clear.]

The following collect and epistle shall be read.

Almighty God, who hast appointed in thy church divers instrumentalities for its edification, and directed by thine apostle that Elders should be ordained in every city, and directed them to feed Thy flock and rule well; and who didst by Thy servants in the beginning of Thy church in Jerusalem, direct Thy congregation to choose out seven men, among whom was Thy martyr Stephen, to serve Thy church, who by the prayer and laying on of the hands of Thy ministers, the apostles, were set apart for their work; mercifully behold these Thy servants whom Thy church have now selected for a like work; replenish them with Thy truth, and fill them with faith and the Holy Spirit, so that they may adorn Thy doctrine by word and innocency of life. May they faithfully fulfil the office whereunto they are called, to Thy glory and the edification of Thy church, through Jesus Christ our Lord. *Amen.*

The Epistle, 1 Tim. iii. 8—13.

Likewise must the Deacons be grave, not double-tongued, not given to much wine, not greedy of filthy lucre; holding the mystery of the faith in a pure conscience. And let these also first be proved; then let them use the office of a Deacon, being found blameless. Even so must their wives be grave, not slanderers, sober, faithful in all things. Let the Deacons be the husband of one wife, ruling their children and their own houses well. For they that have used the office of a Deacon well, purchase to themselves a good degree, and great boldness in the faith, which is in Christ Jesus.

If ruling Elders are to be ordained, read for
The Epistle, Titus i. 4—9.

To Titus, mine own son, after the common faith; grace, mercy, and peace, from God the Father, and the Lord Jesus Christ our Saviour. For this cause left I thee in Crete, that thou shouldst set in order the things that are wanting, and ordain Elders in every city, as I had appointed thee; if any be blameless, the husband of one wife, having faithful children, not accused of riot, or unruly. For a bishop must be blameless, as the steward of God; not self-willed, not soon angry, not given to wine, no striker, not given to filthy lucre, but a lover of hospitality, a lover of good men, sober, just, holy, temperate; holding fast the faithful word as he hath been taught, that he may be able by sound doctrine, both to exhort and convince the gainsayers.

The officiating minister shall then say,—

Beloved Brethren, you have heard from God's most holy and blessed word, the character, duties, and responsibilities of those called to the office to which our Lord, by the voice of his church, has called you. Wherefore, in order that the congregation here present may know your minds in this matter, you will plainly answer to the following questions.

Q. Do you heartily and unfeignedly believe the canonical books of the Old and New Testament?

A. I do believe them.

Q. Will you diligently study and enforce the same, on those whom you are appointed to serve, and also strive to conform your own *life* and *conversation* to the rule given in that word, both as it respects your private life and official character?

A. I will endeavour so to do, the Lord being my helper.

Q. Do you trust that you are inwardly moved by the Holy Spirit to take upon you the office of Deacon (or ruling Elder) in the church of our Lord Jesus, the Messiah, for the edifying of His body, and the glory of God?

A. I trust so.

The officiating minister shall then lay his hands on the head of each candidate (the candidate kneeling) and say,

Take thou authority to exercise the office of a Deacon (or ruling Elder) in the church, in the name of the Father, and of the Son, and of the Holy Spirit. *Amen.*

Let us pray.

Almighty God, giver of every good and perfect gift, who of Thy great mercy hast by Thy Spirit and the voice of Thy church, called *these* Thy *servants* to serve Thee in the holy and important office of Deacons (or Elders) in Thy church, vouchsafe to accept and sanction their consecration to this work by our hands and ministry; make them, we beseech Thee, modest, humble, teachable, and constant in their ministrations, that having always the testimony of a good conscience, and continuing ever strong in the Lord, they may so behave themselves in this their office as that being proved they may purchase to themselves a good degree, and great boldness in the faith, through Jesus Christ our Lord. *Amen.*

The blessing of Almighty God, the Father, the Son, and the Holy Spirit, be among you and remain with you always. *Amen.*

ORDINATION OF MINISTERS.

The candidates elected to ordination for the work of the Gospel ministry, being presented to the officiating minister, the name of each candidate shall be read aloud. This done, the Minister shall say,

Brethren, we propose, this day, to ordain the person (or persons) now presented to us, to the Gospel ministry. After due examination, we find nothing why they are not truly called to this great and holy work, and are not fit persons for the same. But if any of you do know any crime or impediment in any of them why he ought not to be received into this holy ministry, let him now come forth and show it.

[If any impediment be objected to any one the minister shall cease from ordaining him till he shall be cleared.]

THE COLLECT.

Almighty and everlasting God, Thou hast ordained diverse functions of ministry in Thy Church, and by Thy Holy Spirit called and qualified Thy servants to fill the same: mercifully regard these Thy servants called to be ministers of Thy word, and replenish them with Thy truth and adorn them with holiness of life, that they may serve Thee faithfully and honorably in their office, to the glory of Thy most excellent name, and edification of Thy Church; through Jesus Christ our Lord. *Amen.*

THE EPISTLE.—*Ephesians* iv. 7—13.

Unto every one of us is given grace according to the measure of the gift of Christ. Wherefore, he saith, when he ascended up on high, he led captivity captive, and gave gifts unto men. (Now that he ascended, what is it but that he also descended first, into the lower parts of the earth? He that descended, is the same also that ascended up far above all heavens, that he might fill all things.) And he gave some apostles; and some prophets; and some evangelists: and pastors and teachers; for the perfecting of the saints, for the work of the ministry; for the edifying of the body of Christ, till we all come in the unity of the faith, and of the knowledge of the Son of God, unto a perfect man, unto the measure of the stature of the fulness of Christ.

ADDRESS.

When our Lord Jesus Christ ascended up on high, led captivity captive, and received gifts for men, He gave some apostles; some prophets; some evangelists; and some pastors and teachers; for the perfecting of the saints, for the work of the ministry, for the edifying of the body of Christ. Hence, the Gospel ministry is not of man, but the gift and appointment of our Lord Jesus Christ. Nor are we to understand that these various functions imply a different grade of ministry, but rather peculiar gifts bestowed on different individuals of the same order, to meet the wants of the Church. An apostle was one who had personally seen Jesus Christ and received his mission directly from the Head of the Church; as saith Paul: "Am I not an Apostle? Have I not seen Jesus Christ?" And the Gospel he preached, "Was not of man, nor by man, but 'received' by revelation of Jesus Christ." And yet the apostles numbered themselves with the elders, which was the office of all the ministers of the word. Thus Peter declares: "The elders which are among you I exhort, who am also an elder." So likewise, also, were all the elders overseers, or bishops, as expressed by Paul, when he called together the elders of the Church of Ephesus, and declared to them that the Holy Spirit had made them *overseers*, (*episkopoi*) or bishops of the flock of God. The prophets were favored with the direct inspiration of the Holy Spirit, and spoke with the authority of God what was given them, while the evangelists, pastors or teachers, were directed to "*Preach the Word.*" But in office and dignity, they were all elders or bishops, overseers of the flock of God, each to exercise the peculiar gift bestowed on him to accomplish the common end. But each were authorized as fully as the other, to preach the gospel, administer the sacraments, exercise discipline, and ordain others to the same office.

Of how great importance and dignity is the office of this holy ministry!—To be watchmen, messengers of the Lord of hosts, ambassadors of the King of kings, stewards of God's mysteries, shepherds of Christ's flock, workers together with God in saving souls, and preparing a people for the Lord Jesus at His appearing and Kingdom. Wherefore, it is needful that those to whose care so great and valuable a treasure is committed, and of whom so great and important duties are required, should be abundantly endowed with the gifts and graces of the Spirit, to enable them to successfully accomplish their work; and that they should labor in fasting and prayer, with much earnest and careful study, to show themselves approved unto God, workmen that need not be ashamed, rightly dividing the word of truth. For so divine a work must needs require divine aid for its performance.

And that you may have before you, and fully impressed on your mind, the important duties of this holy office, listen to the words of Paul and Peter in their

APOSTOLIC CHARGES.

"Take heed, therefore, unto yourselves, and to all the flock over the which the Holy Ghost hath made you overseers, to feed the Church of God, which he hath purchased with his own blood." "I charge thee, therefore, before God and the Lord Jesus Christ, who shall judge the quick and the dead at his appearing and kingdom; preach the word; be instant in season and out of season; reprove, rebuke, exhort with all long-suffering and doctrine. For the time will come when they will not endure sound doctrine; but after their own lusts shall they heap to themselves teachers, having itching ears, and they shall turn away their ears from the truth, and shall be turned to fables. But watch thou in all things, endure afflictions, do the work of an evangelist, make full proof of thy ministry." "The elders which are among you I exhort, who am also an elder, and a witness of the sufferings of Christ, and also a partaker of the glory that shall be revealed: feed the flock of God which is among you, taking the oversight thereof, not by constraint, but willingly; not for filthy lucre, but of a ready mind; neither as being lords over God's heritage, but being ensamples to the flock. And when the chief shepherd shall appear, ye shall receive a crown of glory that fadeth not away."

We have good hope that long before this, you have well pondered these things in your heart, and have fully determined, by the grace of God, to give yourself wholly to this office, and direct all your cares, labors and studies, to accomplish the ends of the Christian ministry.

And now, that the congregation here present, may understand your determination in this matter, and that your solemn promise may the more move and constrain you to a faithful performance of your duties, you shall answer plainly to these things which we now, in the name of God and His Church, shall demand of you.

QUESTIONS.

Do you trust that you are inwardly moved by the Holy Spirit to take upon you the office and work of the Christian ministry, for the glory of God and the edification of his Church? *I trust so.*

Do you believe the Scriptures of the Old and New Testaments to be the word of God, the only rule of faith and practice? *I do so believe.*

Do you sincerely receive and adopt the Principles of Divine Truth as held and put forth by Messiah's Church, as containing the system of doctrine taught in the Holy Scriptures? *I do thus receive them.*

Do you approve of the government and discipline of Messiah's Church? *I do.*

Do you promise subjection to your brethren in the Lord in your ecclesiastical capacity? *I will be thus subject, the Lord being my helper.*

Have you been induced, as far as you know your own heart, to seek the office of the Holy Ministry from love to God and a sincere desire to promote His glory in the Gospel of his Son? *I trust I have been thus moved.*

Do you promise to be zealous and faithful in maintaining the truths of the Gospel, peace and purity of the Church? *I will, the Lord being my helper.*

Do you engage to be faithful and diligent in the exercise of all private and personal duties, which become you as a Christian and a Minister of the Gospel; as well as in all public and relative duties of your office: endeavoring to walk with exemplary piety before the flock and the world, adorning the profession of the Gospel by your godly conversation? *I will do so, the Lord being my helper.*

Are you willing to take upon you the duties of this great and holy ministry, and to faithfully discharge its duties in the sphere in which the Lord, in his providence, shall call you to act your part, as He shall give you strength? *I will, the Lord being my helper.*

Then shall the presiding Minister say,

Let us Pray.

Almighty God, our Heavenly Father, who hast, at the intercession of Thy well-beloved Son, through the operation of the Holy Spirit, dispensed gifts to men; and for the perfecting of the saints, for the work of the ministry, for the edifying of the body of Christ, hast given apostles, prophets, evangelists, pastors and teachers, look in tender mercy upon Thy *servants* who this day appear before Thee to consecrate themselves to Thy work in the ministry of the Gospel, whereunto we trust Thou hast called them; and grant unto them abundantly the gifts and graces of Thy Holy Spirit to qualify them for their great and important work of laboring for the salvation of mankind. For this great gift of the Christian ministry, for the call of Thy *servants* here present to partake of this ministry, as well as for all the blessings of the Gospel, we praise Thee, we worship Thee, we magnify Thy most excellent and glorious name.

And grant, most merciful God, that through the ministrations of Thy servants, in these last days, so indicative of the speedy consummation of the great work of redemption by the glorious appearing of the Son of Man to receive and establish his everlasting kingdom and dominion under the whole heaven, a multitude of souls may become savingly acquainted with Thee, and be prepared, through grace, to reign with Him in the glory of that kingdom. And grant, unto these Thy servants, grace to endure hardness as good soldiers of Jesus Christ, that they may act faithfully their part as heralds of the Gospel of the kingdom, and that, thus speedily, all nations may hear the joyful tidings and the end of Satan's reign and Zion's sorrow be accomplished; and when the chief Shepherd shall appear, may they, with all Thy faithful ministers, receive a crown of life which fadeth not away; through Thy well-beloved Son, Jesus Christ, to whom, with Thee and the Holy Spirit, be endless praise. *Amen.*

The Ministers present shall then lay their hands severally on the heads of the candidates, (the candidates kneeling) and the officiating Minister shall say,

The Lord pour upon thee the Holy Spirit, for the office and work of a minister in His Church, now committed unto thee by the imposition of our hands. And be thou a faithful dispenser of the word of God, and of His Holy Ordinances; in the name of the Father, and of the Son, and of the Holy Spirit. *Amen.*

Then shall be delivered to each candidate, the Bible, saying,

Take thou authority to preach the word of God and administer the Ordinances of His house.

One of the Ministers, appointed for this purpose, shall give the right hand of fellowship to the ordained.

Our Father, which art in heaven, hallowed be Thy name, Thy kingdom come, thy will be done on earth as it is in heaven: Give us this day our daily bread; forgive us our trespasses as we forgive those who trespass against us; lead us not into temptation, but deliver us from evil; for Thine is the kingdom, the power, and the glory, forever and ever. *Amen.*

The peace of God which passeth all understanding, keep your hearts and minds in the knowledge and love of God, and of his Son, Jesus Christ our Lord; and the blessing of God Almighty, the Father, the Son, and the Holy Spirit, be among you and remain with you always. *Amen.*

DEVOTIONAL HYMNS.

ALPHABETICALLY ARRANGED.

1   C. M.

ALAS! and did my Saviour bleed,
  And did my Sovereign die?
Would he devote that sacred head
  For such a worm as I?

2 Was it for crimes that I have done,
  He groan'd upon the tree?
Amazing pity! grace unknown!
  And love beyond degree!

3 Well might the sun in darkness hide,
  And shut his glories in;
When Christ, the mighty Maker, died
  For man the creature's sin!

4 Thus might I hide my blushing face,
  While his dear cross appears:
Dissolve my heart in thankfulness,
  And melt mine eyes to tears.

5 But drops of grief can ne'er repay
  The debt of love I owe:
Here, Lord, I give myself away,
  'Tis all that I can do.

2   C. M.

ALL hail the power of Jesus' name!
  Let angels prostrate fall;
Bring forth the royal diadem,
  And crown him Lord of all.

2 Ye chosen seed of Israel's race,
  A remnant weak and small!
Hail him who saves you by his grace,
  And crown him Lord of all.

3 Ye Gentile sinners, ne'er forget
  The wormwood and the gall;
Go, spread your trophies at his feet,
  And crown him Lord of all.

4 May we with heaven's rejoicing throng
  Before his presence fall,
Join in the everlasting song,
  And crown him Lord of all!

3   C. M.

AM I a soldier of the cross,
  A follower of the Lamb?
And shall I fear to own his cause,
  Or blush to speak his name?

2 Shall I be carried to the skies
  On flowery beds of ease?
While others fought to win the prize,
  And sailed through bloody seas.

3 Are there no foes for me to face,
  Must I not stem the flood?
Is this vain world a friend to grace,
  To help me on to God?

4 Sure I must fight if I would reign,
   Increase my courage, Lord!
I'll bear the toil, endure the pain,
   Supported by thy word.

5 Thy saints in all this glorious war
   Shall conquer though they die;
They see the triumph from afar,
   By faith they bring it nigh.

6 When that illustrious day shall rise,
   And all thy armies shine
In robes of victory through the skies,
   The glory shall be thine.

4   S. M.

AND are we yet alive,
   And see each other's face?
Glory and praise to Jesus give,
   For his redeeming grace.
Preserved by power divine
   To full salvation here,
Again in Jesus' praise we join,
   And in his sight appear.

2 What troubles have we seen!
   What conflicts have we pass'd!
Fightings without, and fears within,
   Since we assembled last!
But out of all the Lord
   Hath brought us by his love;
And still he doth his help afford,
   And hides our life above.

5   L. P. M.

AND can it be that I should gain
  An int'rest in the Saviour's blood?
Died he for me, who caused his pain?
  For me, who him to death pursued?
Amazing love! how can it be,
That thou, my Lord, shouldst die for me?

2 'Tis myst'ry all—th' Immortal dies!
  Who can explore his strange design?
In vain the first-born seraph tries
  To sound the depths of love divine;
'Tis mercy all! let earth adore:
Let angel minds inquire no more.

3 He left his Father's throne above;
  (So free, so infinite his grace!)
Emptied himself of all but love,
  And bled for Adam's helpless race:
'Tis mercy all, immense and free,
For, O my God, it found out me!

6   C. M.

AND must I be to judgment brought,
  And answer in that day
For every vain and idle thought,
  And every word I say?

2 Yes, every secret of my heart
  Shall shortly be made known,
And I receive my just desert
  For all that I have done.

3 How careful then ought I to live;
  With what religious fear;

Who such a strict account must give
  For my behaviour here.

4 Thou awful Judge of quick and dead,
  The watchful power bestow;
So shall I to my ways take heed,—
  To all I speak or do.

5 If now thou standest at the door,
  O let me feel thee near;
And make my peace with God, before
  I at thy bar appear.

8   8s, 7s, 4s.

ANGELS now are hov'ring round us,
  Unperceiv'd they mix the throng,
Wond'ring at the love that crown'd us,
  Glad to join the holy song:
Hallelujah! Hallelujah!
  Love and praise to Christ belong!

2 Now I see with joy and wonder,
  Whence the gracious spring arose;
Angel minds are lost to ponder,
  Dying love's mysterious cause;
Yet the blessing, Yet the blessing,
  Down to all, to me it flows!

3 This hath set me all on fire;
  Strongly glows the flame of love;
Higher mounts my soul, and higher,
  Struggles for its swift remove;
Then I'll praise him, Then I'll praise him,
  In a nobler strain above!

9   S. M.

ANGELS our march oppose,
  Who still in strength excel,—
Our secret, sworn, eternal foes,
  Countless, invisible;
From thrones of glory driven,
  By flaming vengeance hurl'd,
They throng the air, and darken heaven,
  And rule this lower world.

2 But shall believers fear?
  But shall believers fly?
Or see the bloody cross appear,
  And all their powers defy?
By all hell's host withstood,
  We all hell's host o'erthrow;
And, conqu'ring them through Jesus' blood,
  We on to conquer go.

10   H. M.

ARISE, my soul, arise!
  Shake off thy guilty fears;
The bleeding sacrifice
  In my behalf appears;
Before the throne my Saviour stands;
My name is written on his hands.

2 He ever lives above,
  For me to intercede;
His all-redeeming love,
  His precious blood to plead;
His blood atoned for all our race,
And sprinkles now the throne of grace.

3 The bleeding wounds he bears,
   Received on Calvary,
They pour effectual prayers,
   They strongly speak for me.
Forgive him, O forgive, they cry,
Nor let that ransomed sinner die!

4 The Father hears him pray,
   His dear anointed One;
He cannot turn away
   The presence of his Son;
His Spirit answers to the blood,
And tells me I am born of God.

5 To God I'm reconciled;
   His pardoning voice I hear;
He owns me for his child;
   I can no longer fear;
With confidence I now draw nigh,
And Father, Abba, Father, cry.

11   P. M.

AS I view the last sands of old time sink away,
   O grant me, dear Saviour, this boon:
That I never, never may from thy smiles go astray,
   Nor share the impenitent's doom.

CHORUS.

Roll on, then, old time, while I sigh for the land,
   Through this dark, gloomy region of pain,
For fair Beulah's land, and the pure spotless band,
   Where the King in his beauty shall reign.

2 Pilgrim, haste on thy way, for the sun's gliding down;
   Escape for thy life, while there's room;

See dark clouds gath'ring round, mantling earth
    with a frown,
  And wide spreads the thick'ning gloom.

3 Pilgrim, hark, on each breeze as it comes from
    afar,
  How the low mutt'ring thunders break round!
From the dim distant shore rings the clarion of
    war,
  Haste thee on! soon the last trump shall sound!

4 Pilgrim, lift up thy head, soon the kingdom
    will come,
  And the saints then in glory appear;
In their fair Eden home, with their King ever
  And his hand wipe away every tear. [roam,

12   C. M.

ATTEND, O earth! God doth declare
    His uncontrolled decree;
"Thou art my Son, this day, my heir,
    Have I begotten thee.

2 "Upon my holy Zion's hill
    My King I thee ordain;
And though thy foes dispute my will,
    Thou shalt forever reign.

3 "Ask, and receive thy full demands;
    Thine shall the heathen be;
The utmost limit of the lands
    Shall be possessed by thee."

13   C. M.

ATTEND, and mark the solemn fast
   Which to the Lord is dear;
Disdain the false, unhallowed mask
   Which vain dissemblers wear.

2 Do I delight in sorrow's dress?
   Saith he who reigns above;
The hanging head and rueful look,
   Will they attract my love?

3 Let such as feel oppression's load
   Thy tender pity share;
And let the helpless, homeless poor
   Be thy peculiar care.

4 Go, bid the hungry orphan be
   With thy abundance blessed;
Invite the wanderer to thy gate,
   And spread the couch of rest.

5 Let him who pines with piercing cold
   By thee be warmed and clad;
Be thine the blissful task to make
   The downcast mourner glad.

6 Then, bright as morning, shall come forth,
   In peace and joy, thy days;
And glory from the Lord above
   Shall shine on all thy ways.

14   C. M.

AUTHOR of faith, eternal Word,
   Whose Spirit breathes the active flame;
Faith, like its finisher and Lord,
   To-day, as yesterday, the same:—

2 To thee our humble hearts aspire,
   And ask the gift unspeakable;
Increase in us the kindled fire,
   In us the work of faith fulfil.

3 By faith we know thee strong to save:
   (Save us, a present Saviour thou:)
Whate'er we hope, by faith we have;
   Future and past, subsisting now.

4 To him that in thy Name believes,
   Eternal life with thee is given;
Into himself he all receives,—
   Pardon, and holiness, and heaven.

5 The things unknown to feeble sense,
   Unseen by reason's glimm'ring ray,
With strong commanding evidence,
   Their heavenly origin display.

6 Faith lends its realizing light;
   The clouds disperse, the shadows fly;
Th' Invisible appears in sight,
   And God is seen by mortal eye.

15   8s.

AWAY with our sorrow and fear;
   We soon shall recover our home;
The city of saints shall appear;
   The day of eternity come.

2 Our mourning is all at an end,
   When, raised by the life-giving word,
We see the new city descend,
   Adorned as a bride for her Lord.

3 By faith we already behold
   That lovely Jerusalem here;
Her walls are of jasper and gold,
   As crystal her buildings are clear.

4 The saints in God's presence receive
   Their great and eternal reward;
With Jesus forever they live,
   And reign on the earth with their Lord.

16   L. M.

BEFORE Jehovah's awful throne,
   Ye nations bow, with sacred joy;
Know that the Lord is God alone;
   He can create, and he destroy.

2 His sovereign power, without our aid,
   Made us of clay, and formed us men;
And when like wandering sheep we strayed,
   He brought us to his fold again.

3 We'll crowd thy gates with thankful songs;
   High as the heavens our voices raise;
And earth with her ten thousand tongues
   Shall fill thy courts with sounding praise.

4 Wide as the world is thy command;
   Vast as eternity thy love;
Firm as a rock thy truth must stand
   When rolling years shall cease to move.

17   C. M.

BEHOLD what condescending love
   Jesus on earth displays!—
To babes and sucklings he extends
   The riches of his grace.

2 He still the ancient promise keeps,
  To our forefathers given ;
Young children in his arms he takes,
  And calls them heirs of heaven.

3 Forbid them not, whom Jesus calls,
  Nor dare the claim resist,
Since his own lips to us declare
  Of such will heaven consist.

4 With flowing tears, and thankful hearts,
  We give them up to thee ;
Receive them, Lord, into thine arms;
  Thine may they ever be.

18 C. M.

BEHOLD the Saviour of mankind
  Nail'd to the shameful tree ;
How vast the love that him inclined
  To bleed and die for thee !

2 Hark ! how he groans, while nature shakes,
  And earth's strong pillars bends :
The temple's veil in sunder breaks,—
  The solid marbles rends.

3 'Tis done ! the precious ransom's paid !
  Receive my soul ! he cries :
See where he bows his sacred head ;
  He bows his head, and dies.

4 But soon he'll break death's envious chain,
  And in full glory shine :
O Lamb of God, was ever pain,
  Was ever love, like thine ?

19   S. M.

BLEST be the tie that binds
  Our hearts in Christian love;
The fellowship of kindred minds
  Is like to that above.

2 Before our Father's throne,
  We pour our ardent prayers;
Our fears, our hopes, our aims are one,—
  Our comforts and our cares.

3 We share our mutual woes;
  Our mutual burdens bear;
And often for each other flows
  The sympathizing tear.

4 When we asunder part,
  It gives us inward pain;
But we shall still be join'd in heart,
  And hope to meet again.

20   H. M.

BLOW, ye the trumpet, blow
  The gladly-solemn sound;
Let all the nations know,
  To earth's remotest bound,
The year of jubilee is come;
Return, ye ransom'd sinners, home.

2 Jesus, our great High Priest,
  Hath full atonement made:
Ye weary spirits, rest;
  Ye mournful souls be glad:
The year of jubilee is come;
Return, ye ransom'd sinners, home.

3 Extol the Lamb of God,—
    The all-atoning Lamb;
Redemption in his blood
    Throughout the world proclaim:
The year of jubilee is come;
Return, ye ransom'd sinners, home.

6 The gospel trumpet hear,—
    The news of heavenly grace;
And, saved from earth, appear
    Before your Saviour's face:
The year of jubilee is come;
Return, ye ransom'd sinners, home.

21   7s.

BRETHREN, while we sojourn here,
    Fight we must, but should not fear;
Foes we have, but we've a Friend,
One that loves us to the end:
Forward, then, with courage go,
Long we shall not dwell below;
Soon the joyful news will come,
"Child, your Father calls, Come home."

2 In the way a thousand snares
Lie to take us unawares;
Satan, with malicious art,
Watches each unguarded heart:
But from Satan's malice free,
Saints shall soon in glory be;
Soon the joyful news will come,
"Child, your Father calls, Come home."

22   P. M.

BY faith I see my Saviour dying,
  On the tree, on the tree;
To every nation he is crying,
  Look to me, look to me;
He bids the guilty now draw near,
Repent, believe, dismiss your fear
Hark! hark! what precious words I hear,
  Mercy's free, mercy's free.

2 Did Christ, when I was sin pursuing,
  Pity me, pity me?
And did he snatch my soul from ruin,
  Can it be, can it be?
Oh yes! he did salvation bring,
He is my Prophet, Priest and King,
And now my happy soul can sing,
  Mercy's free, mercy's free.

23   7s.

CHILDREN of the heavenly King!
  As ye journey, sweetly sing;
Sing your Saviour's worthy praise,
Glorious in his works and ways.

CHORUS.

Victory! victory!
When we've gained the victory;
O how happy we shall be,
When we've gained the victory.

2 Ye are travelling home to God,
In the way the fathers trod;
They are happy now, and ye
Soon their happiness shall see.

3. Shout, ye little flock, and blest;
You on Jesus' throne shall rest;
There, your seat is now prepared,—
There, your kingdom and reward.

4 Fear not, brethren, joyful stand
On the borders of your land;
Jesus Christ, your Father's Son,
Bids you undismayed go on.

24   7s.

CHRISTIANS, brethren, ere we part,
  Every voice and every heart
Join, and to our Father raise
One last hymn of grateful praise.

2 Though we here should meet no more,
Yet there is a brighter shore:
There, released from toil and pain,
There we all may meet again.

25   P.M.

CHRISTIAN, the warfare will now soon be
  O do not fear, do not fear! [o'er;
Soon thou wilt rest where thy foes come no
  Be of good cheer, of good cheer! [more;
What though the night be so dreary and long?
What though thy foes are unwearied and strong?
Soon thou shalt join in the conqueror's song:
  Be of good cheer, of good cheer!

2 What though the billows of life darkly roll?
  O do not fear, do not fear!
Friends all forsake thee, and cares press thy
  Be of good cheer, of good cheer! [soul?

Christian, remember that Christ loves thee still;
Only be faithful in doing his will;
Soon thou wilt stand with him on Zion's hill:
  Be of good cheer, of good cheer!

26   P. M.

COME and reign; come and reign,
  Jesus on thy throne;
And, O, it fills my heart with joy
  To know we're almost home.
Here I drop the falling tear,
  As pilgrim-like I roam,
An exile from my Father's house;
  But soon he'll call me home.

2 Here amid life's changing scenes,
  My cup of grief runs o'er;
But there I'll share unmingled bliss
  On Canaan's happy shore.

3 Here I grieve the friends I love,
  And they in turn grieve me;
But O, my Father, grant me grace,
  That I may not grieve thee.

4 Here disease invades our frames,
  We wither, droop, and die;
But there eternal youth shall bloom,
  And bright shall beam each eye.

5 Here we meet and part again,
  As round and round we roam;
But there we'll meet and part no more,
  And sweetly rest at home.

27
7s.

COME, Desire of nations, come!
  Hasten, Lord, the general doom!
Hear the Spirit and the Bride;
Come, and take us to thy side.

2 Thou, who hast our place prepared,
Make us meet for our reward;
Then with all thy saints descend;
Then our earthly trials end.

3 Mindful of thy chosen race,
Shorten these vindictive days;
Who for full redemption groan:
Hear us now, and save thine own.

4 Now destroy the Man of sin;
Now thine ancient flock bring in;
Filled with righteousness divine,
Claim a ransomed world for thine.

5 Plant thy heavenly kingdom here;
Glorious in thy saints appear;
Speak the sacred number sealed,
Speak the mystery revealed.

6 Take to thee thy royal power;
Reign, when sin shall be no more;
Reign, when death no more shall be;
Reign to all eternity.

28
C. M.

COME, Holy Ghost, our hearts inspire;
  Let us thine influence prove;—
Source of the old prophetic fire;
  Fountain of life and love.

2 Come, Holy Ghost, for moved by thee
   The prophets wrote and spoke:
Unlock the truth, thyself the key;
   Unseal the sacred book.

3 Expand thy wings, Celestial Dove;
   Brood o'er our nature's night;
On our disorder'd spirits move,
   And let there now be light.

4 God, through himself, we then shall know,
   If thou within us shine;
And sound, with all thy saints below,
   The depths of love divine.

29   C. M.

COME, Holy Spirit, heavenly Dove,
   With all thy quick'ning powers;
Kindle a flame of sacred love
   In these cold hearts of ours.

2 Look how we grovel here below,
   Fond of these earthly toys;
Our souls, how heavily they go,
   To reach eternal joys.

3 In vain we tune our formal songs,—
   In vain we strive to rise;
Hosannas languish on our tongues,
   And our devotion dies.

4 Father, and shall we ever live
   At this poor dying rate:
Our love so faint, so cold to thee,
   And thine to us so great?

5 Come, Holy Spirit, heavenly Dove,
  With all thy quick'ning powers;
Come, shed abroad a Saviour's love,
  And that shall kindle ours.

30   P. M.

COME, let us anew our journey pursue,
  Roll round with the year,
And never stand still till the Master appear.
His adorable will let us gladly fulfil,
  And our talents improve,
By the patience of hope, and the labour of love.

2 Our life is a dream; our time as a stream,
  Glides swiftly away,
And the fugitive moment refuses to stay.
The arrow is flown,—the moment is gone;
  The millennial year
Rushes on to our view, and eternity's here.

3 O that each, in the day of His coming, may
  I have fought my way through; [say,—
I have finished the work thou didst give me to do.
O that each from his Lord may receive the glad
  Well and faithfully done! [word,—
Enter into my joy, and sit down on my throne.

31   C. M.

COME, let us join our cheerful songs
  With angels round the throne;
Ten thousand thousand are their tongues,
  But all their joys are one.

2 Worthy the Lamb that died, they cry,
  To be exalted thus:

Worthy the Lamb, our hearts reply,
   For he was slain for us.

3 Jesus is worthy to receive
   Honour and power divine;
And blessings more than we can give,
   Be, Lord, forever thine.

4 The whole creation join in one,
   To bless the sacred Name
Of Him that sits upon the throne,
   And to adore the Lamb.

32   C. M.

COME, let us use the grace divine,
   And all, with one accord,
In a perpetual cov'nant join
   Ourselves to Christ the Lord;—

2 Give up ourselves, through Jesus' power,
   His name to glorify;
And promise, in this sacred hour,
   For God to live and die.

3 The cov'nant we this moment make
   Be ever kept in mind;
We will no more our God forsake,
   Or cast his words behind.

4 We never will throw off his fear,
   Who hears our solemn vow;
And if thou art well pleased to hear,
   Come down, and meet us now.

6

33 7s.

COMING Saviour, now in faith,
  We remember still thy death;
Thou wast broken, thou hast died,
For us thou wast crucified.

2 While in faith we drink the wine,
Of thy blood we see the sign;
Wash us pure from every stain,
Thou that comest soon to reign.

3 Lord, we thus remember thee;
But we long thy face to see,
Long to reach our heavenly home;
"Come, Lord Jesus, quickly come!"

4 Quickly thou thyself wilt come;
Thou wilt raise us to thy throne,
And thy glories here display
Through the never-ending day.

34 C. M.

COME, Saviour, let thy tokens prove,
  Fitted by heavenly art,
As channels to convey thy love,
  To every faithful heart.

2 The living bread, sent down from heaven,
  In us vouchsafe to be;
Thy flesh for all the world is given,
  And all may live by thee.

3 Now, Lord, on us thy flesh bestow,
  And let us drink thy blood,
Till all our souls are filled, below,
  With all the life of God.

4 Determined nothing else to know
   But Jesus crucified,
We will not from our Jesus go,
   Or leave his wounded side.

35   C. M.

COME, trembling sinner, in whose breast
   A thousand thoughts revolve;
Come, with your guilt and fear oppressed,
   And make this last resolve:

2 I'll go to Jesus, though my sin
   Hath like a mountain rose;
I know his courts, I'll enter in,
   Whatever may oppose.

3 Perhaps he will admit my plea,
   Perhaps will hear my prayer;
But if I perish, I will pray,
   And perish only there.

4 I can but perish if I go;
   I am resolved to try;
For if I stay away, I know
   I must forever die.

36   S. M.

COME, we that love the Lord,
   And let our joys be known;
Join in a song with sweet accord,
And thus surround the throne.

2 The sorrows of the mind
   Be banished from the place;
Religion never was designed
   To make our pleasures less.

3 The men of grace have found
    Glory begun below;
Celestial fruits on earthly ground,
    From faith and hope may grow.

5 There we shall see his face,
    And never, never sin;
There, from the rivers of his grace,
    Drink endless pleasures in.

37   8s. 7s. 4s.

COME, ye sinners, poor and needy,
    Weak and wounded, sick and sore;
Jesus ready stands to save you,
    Full of mercy, love, and power.
        He is able,
He is willing; doubt no more.

2 Ho! ye needy, come and welcome,
    God's free bounty glorify;
True belief, and true repentance,
    Every grace that brings us nigh.
        Without money,
Come to Jesus Christ, and buy.

3 Let not conscience make you linger,
    Nor of fitness fondly dream!
All the fitness he requireth
    Is to feel your need of him.
        This he gives you,
'Tis the Spirit's rising beam.

4 Come, ye weary, heavy-laden,
    Lost and ruined by the fall,
If you tarry till you're better,
    You will never come at all.
        Not the righteous,
Sinners, Jesus came to call.

5 Lo! the incarnate God, ascended,
   Pleads the merit of his blood,
Venture on him, venture wholly,
   Let no other trust intrude;
     None but Jesus
Can do helpless sinners good.

38   H. M.

COME, ye who love the Lord,
   And feel his quick'ning power,
Unite with one accord,
   His goodness to adore;
To heaven and earth aloud proclaim
Your great Redeemer's glorious name!

2 He left his throne above,
   His glory laid aside,
Came down on wings of love,
   And wept, and bled, and died:
The pangs he bore, what tongue can tell,
To save our souls from death and hell?

3 He burst the grave; he rose
   Victorious from the dead;
And thence his vanquished foes
   In glorious triumph led:
Up through the heavens the Conq'ror rode
Triumphant to the throne of God.

4 He soon again will come,
   His chariot will not stay,
To take his children home
   To realms of endless day:
We there shall see him face to face,
And sing the triumphs of his grace.

39
S. M.

COME, sinners, to the gospel feast;
  Let every soul be Jesus' guest:
Ye need not one be left behind,
For God hath bidden all mankind.

2 Sent by my Lord, on you I call;
The invitation is to all:—
Come all the world! come, sinner, thou!
All things in Christ are ready now.

3 Come, all ye souls by sin oppress'd,
Ye restless wand'rers after rest;
Ye poor, and maim'd, and halt, and blind,
In Christ a hearty welcome find.

4 My message as from God receive;
Ye all may come to Christ and live:
O let his love your hearts constrain,
Nor suffer him to die in vain.

40
C. M.

COME, O my God, the promise seal,
  This mountain, sin, remove;
Now in my waiting soul reveal
  The virtue of thy love.

2 I want thy life, thy purity,
  Thy righteousness, brought in:
I ask, desire, and trust in thee
  To be redeem'd from sin.

3 For this, as taught by thee, I pray,
  My inbred sin cast out:
Thou wilt, in me, thy power display;
  I can no longer doubt.

4 Let anger, sloth, desire, and pride,
   This moment be subdued;
Be cast into the crimson tide
   Of my Redeemer's blood.

5 'Tis done; thou dost this moment save—
   With full salvation bless;
Redemption through thy blood I have,
   And spotless love and peace.

41   L. P. M.

COME, O thou Traveller unknown,
   Whom still I hold, but cannot see;
My company before is gone,
   And I am left alone with thee:
With thee all night I mean to stay,
And wrestle till the break of day.

2 I need not tell thee who I am;
   My sin and misery declare;
Thyself hast call'd me by my name;
   Look on thy hands, and read it there:
But who, I ask thee, who art thou?
Tell me thy name, and tell me now.

3 In vain thou strugglest to get free;
   I never will unloose my hold:
Art thou the Man that died for me?
   The secret of thy love unfold:
Wrestling, I will not let thee go,
Till I thy name, thy nature know.

42   S. M.

COME, sound his praise abroad,
   And hymns of glory sing:
Jehovah is the sov'reign God,
   The universal king,

2 He form'd the deeps unknown;
  He gave the seas their bound;
The wat'ry worlds are all his own,
  And all the solid ground.

3 Come, worship at his throne,
  Come, bow before the Lord;
We are his works, and not our own,
  He form'd us by his word.

4 To-day attend his voice,
  Nor dare provoke his rod;
Come, like the people of his choice,
  And own your gracious God.

43   L. M.

COME, tune, ye saints, your noblest strains,
  Your dying, risen Lord to sing;
And echo, to the heavenly plains,
  The triumphs of your Saviour King.

2 In songs of grateful rapture tell
  How he subdued your potent foes;
Subdued the powers of death and hell,
  And, dying, finished all your woes.

3 Then to his glorious throne on high
  Returned, while hymning angels round,
Through the bright arches of the sky,
  The Lord, the conquering Lord, resound.

4 Almighty love! victorious power!
  Not angel tongues can e'er display
The wonders of that dreadful hour—
  The joys of that illustrious day.

5 Dear Saviour, let thy wondrous grace
  Fill every heart, and every tongue;
Till the full glories of thy face
  Inspire a sweeter, nobler song.

44   7s.

DEPTH of mercy! can there be
  Mercy still reserved for me?
Can my God his wrath forbear?
Me, the chief of sinners, spare?

2 I have long withstood his grace;
Long provoked him to his face;
Would not hearken to his calls;
Grieved him by a thousand falls.

3 Now incline me to repent;
Let me now my sins lament;
Now my soul revolt deplore,
Weep, believe, and sin no more.

4 Kindled his relentings are;
Me he now delights to spare;
Cries, How shall I give thee up?—
Lets the lifted thunder drop.

5 There for me the Saviour stands;
Shows his wounds, and spreads his hands;
God is love! I know, I feel;
Jesus weeps, and loves me still.

45   H. M.

DOWN from the willow-bough
  My slumbering harp I'll take,
And bid its silent strings
  To heavenly themes awake:
How peaceful should its breathings be,
Dear Saviour, when I sing of thee!

2 Love, Love on earth appears;
   The wretched throng his way;
He beareth all their griefs,
   And wipes their tears away;
How soft and sweet the strain should be
Whene'er I sing of Calvary!

3 "I die for thee," he said,
   Behold the cross arise;
And lo, he bows his head,
   He bows his head and dies!
Soft, soft, my harp, thy breathings be!
Here let me weep on Calvary.

46   L. M.

ETERNAL Power, whose high abode
   Becomes the grandeur of a God:
Infinite lengths, beyond the bounds
Where stars revolve their little rounds:

2 Thee while the first archangel sings,
He hides his face behind his wings:
And ranks of shining thrones around
Fall worshipping, and spread the ground.

3 Lord, what shall earth and ashes do?
We would adore our Maker too;
From sin and dust to thee we cry,
The Great, the Holy, and the High.

4 Earth, from afar, hath heard thy fame,
And worms have learn'd to lisp thy name;
But O! the glories of thy mind
Leave all our soaring thoughts behind.

5 God is in heaven, and men below:
Be short our tunes; our words be few:
A solemn rev'rence check our songs,
And praise sits silent on our tongues.

47   L. M.

FAR from my thoughts, vain world, begone,
   Let my religious hours alone:
From flesh and sense I would be free,
And hold communion, Lord, with thee.

2 My heart grows warm with holy fire,
And kindles with a pure desire
To see thy grace, to taste thy love,
And feel thy influence from above.

48   C. M.

FATHER, how wide thy glory shines,
   How high thy wonders rise!
Known through the earth by thousand signs,
   By thousands through the skies.

2 Those mighty orbs proclaim thy power;
   Their motions speak thy skill:
And on the wings of every hour
   We read thy patience still.

3 Part of thy Name divinely stands,
   On all thy creatures writ;
They show the labour of thy hands,
   Or impress of thy feet:

4 But when we view thy strange design
   To save rebellious worms,
Where vengeance and compassion join
   In their divinest forms:

5 Here the whole Deity is known,
   Nor dares a creature guess
Which of the glories brighter shone,
   The justice or the grace.

49   7s.

FATHER, Son, and Holy Ghost,
   One in Three, and Three in One,
As by the celestial host,
   Let thy will on earth be done;
Praise by all to thee be given,
Glorious Lord of earth and heaven.

2 If so poor a worm as I
   May to thy great glory live,
All my actions sanctify,
   All my words and thoughts receive;
Claim me for thy service, claim
All I have, and all I am.

3 Take my soul and body's powers;
   Take my mem'ry, mind, and will;
All my goods, and all my hours;
   All I know, and all I feel;
All I think, or speak, or do;
Take my heart, but make it new.

50   S. M.

"FOR ever with the Lord!"
   Amen, so let it be;
Life for the dead is in that word,
   'Tis immortality.
Here in the body pent,

Absent from Him I roam;
Yet nightly pitch my moving tent
　A day's march nearer home,
Nearer home, nearer home,
A day's march nearer home.

2 My father's house on high,
　　Home of my soul, how near
At times, to faith's aspiring eye,
　　Thy golden gates appear!
Ah, then my spirit faints,
　　To reach the land I love;
The bright inheritance of saints,
　　Jerusalem above.

51   L. M.

FROM every stormy wind that blows,
　From every swelling tide of woes,
There is a calm, a sure retreat,
'Tis found beneath the mercy-seat.

2 There is a place where Jesus sheds
The oil of gladness on our heads;
A place of all on earth most sweet;
It is the blood-bought mercy-seat.

3 There is a scene where spirits blend,
Where friend holds fellowship with friend;
Though sundered far, by faith they meet
Around one common mercy-seat.

4 There, there, on eagle's wings we soar,
And sin and sense molest no more;
And heaven comes down our souls to greet,
And glory crowns the mercy-seat.

52 C. M.

From whence doth this union arise,
  That hatred is conquered by love?
It fastens our souls in such ties
  That nature and time can't remove.

2 It cannot in Eden be found,
  Nor yet in a paradise lost;
It grows on Immanuel's ground,
  And Jesus' dear blood it did cost.

3 Why then so unwilling to part,
  Since we shall ere long meet again?
Engraved on Immanuel's heart,
  At distance we cannot remain.

4 And when we shall see the bright day,
  When Jesus descends from above,
And angels his glory display,
  We then to his kingdom remove.

5 With Jesus we ever shall reign,
  And all his rich glory shall see;
Then sing Hallelujah, Amen!
  Amen, even so let it be!

53 L. M.

From all that dwell below the skies,
  Let the Creator's praise arise;
Let the Redeemer's name be sung,
Through every land, by every tongue.

2 Eternal are thy mercies, Lord;
Eternal truth attends thy word:
Thy praise shall sound from shore to shore,
Till suns shall rise and set no more.

3 Your lofty themes, ye mortals, bring;
In songs of praise divinely sing;
The great salvation loud proclaim,
And shout for joy the Saviour's name.

4 In every land begin the song;
To every land the strains belong:
In cheerful sounds all voices raise,
And fill the world with loudest praise.

54   L. M.

GO, preach the gospel, saith the Lord;
   Bid the whole world my grace receive;
He shall be saved who trusts my word,
   And he condemned who won't believe.

2 I'll make your great commission known;
   And ye shall prove my gospel true,
By all the works that I have done,
   By all the wonders ye shall do.

3 Teach all the nations my commands;
   I'm with you till the world shall end;
All power is trusted in my hands;
   I can destroy, and I defend.

55   L. M.

GREAT God, indulge my humble claim;
   Be thou my hope, my joy, my rest;
The glories that compose thy name
   Stand all engaged to make me blest.

2 Thou great and good, thou just and wise,
   Thou art my Father and my God;
And I am thine by sacred ties,—
   Thy son, thy servant bought with blood.

3 With heart and eyes, and lifted hands,
   For thee I long, to thee I look;
As travellers in thirsty lands
   Pant for the cooling water-brook.

4 I'll lift my hands, I'll raise my voice,
   While I have breath to pray or praise:
This work shall make my heart rejoice,
   And fill the remnant of my days.

56   S. M.

GREAT God, now condescend
   To bless our rising race;
Soon may their willing spirits bend,
   The subjects of thy grace.

2 O what a pure delight
   Their happiness to see;
Our warmest wishes all unite,
   To lead their souls to thee.

3 Now bless, thou God of love,
   This ordinance divine;
Send thy good Spirit from above,
   And make these children thine.

57   L. M.

GREAT God of nations, now to thee
   Our hymn of gratitude we raise;
With humble heart, and bending knee,
   We offer thee our song of praise.

2 Thy Name we bless, almighty God,
   For all the kindness thou hast shown
To this fair land the pilgrims trod,—
   This land we fondly call our own.

3 Here freedom spreads her banner wide,
   And casts her soft and hallow'd ray;
Here thou our fathers' steps didst guide
   In safety through their dang'rous way.

4 We praise thee that the gospel's light
   Through all our land its radiance sheds;
Dispels the shades of error's night,
   And heavenly blessings round us spreads.

5 Great God, preserve us in thy fear;
   In danger still our guardian be;
O, spread thy truth's bright precepts here;
   Let all the people worship thee.

58   C. M.

HARK! from the tombs a doleful sound;
   My ears, attend the cry:—
Ye living men, come view the ground
   Where you must shortly lie.

2 Princes, this clay must be your bed,
   In spite of all your towers;
The tall, the wise, the reverend head,
   Shall lie as low as ours.

3 Great God! is this our certain doom,
   And are we still secure?
Still walking downward to the tomb,
   And yet prepared no more?

4 Grant us the power of quick'ning grace,
   To fit our souls to fly;
Then when we drop this dying flesh,
   We'll rise above the sky.

59   8s, 4s.

HARK! how the Gospel trumpet sounds!
   Through all the world the echo bounds,
And Jesus, by redeeming blood,
Is bringing sinners back to God:
And guides them safely by his word
   To endless day.

2 Hail! all-victorious, conqu'ring Lord!
Be thou by all thy works ador'd,
Who undertook for sinful man,
And brought salvation through thy name,
That we with thee may ever reign
   In endless day.

3 Fight on, ye conqu'ring souls, fight on!
And when the conquest you have won,
Then palms of vict'ry you shall bear,
And in his kingdom have a share;
And crowns of glory ever wear
   In endless day.

60   P. M.

HARK, ten thousand harps and voices
   Sound the notes of praise above;
Jesus reigns, and heaven rejoices;
   Jesus reigns, the God of love:
See, he sits on yonder throne;
Jesus rules the world alone.
   Hallelujah, hallelujah, hallelujah, Amen!

2 Jesus, hail, whose glory brightens
   All above, and gives it worth;
Lord of life, thy smile enlightens,
   Cheers and charms thy saints on earth;

When we think of love like thine,
Lord, we own it love divine.
Hallelujah, hallelujah, hallelujah, Amen!

61   7s.

HARK! the song of jubilee,
  Loud as mighty thunders roar,
Or the fulness of the sea
  When it breaks upon the shore.

2 Hallelujah! for the Lord
  God Omnipotent shall reign;
Hallelujah! let the word
  Echo round the earth and main.

3 See Jehovah's banner furled,
  Sheathed his sword, he speaks, 'tis done,
And the kingdoms of this world
  Are the kingdoms of his Son.

4 He shall reign from pole to pole,
  With illimitable sway:
He shall reign when like a scroll
  Yonder heavens shall pass away.

62   P. M.

HASTE, my dull soul, arise,
  Shake off thy care;
Press to thy native skies,
  Mighty in prayer.
Christ, he has gone before,
Count all thy sufferings o'er,
He all thy burdens bore—
  Jesus is there.

2 Souls for the marriage feast
   Robed and prepared;
Holy must be such guests:
   Jesus is there!
Saints, wear your victory palms,
Chant your celestial psalms;
Bride of the Lamb, thy charms
   O, let me wear!

3 Heaven's bliss is perfect, pure,
   Jesus is there!
Heaven's bliss is ever sure,
   Thou art its heir.
What makes its joys complete?
What makes its hymns so sweet?
There we our friends will greet:
   Jesus is there!

63   7s, 6s.

HAIL to the Lord's anointed,
   Great David's greater Son,
Hail in the time appointed,
   His reign on earth begun!
He comes to break oppression,
   To set the captive free;
To take away transgression,
   And rule in equity.

2 He comes with succour speedy
   To those who suffer wrong;
To help the poor and needy,
   And bid the weak be strong;
To give them songs for sighing,
   Their darkness turn to light,
Whose souls, condemned and dying,
   Were precious in his sight.

64   S. M.

HOW beauteous are their feet,
  Who stand on Zion's hill;
That bring salvation on their tongues,
  And words of peace reveal!

2 How charming is their voice,
  So sweet the tidings are;
"Zion, behold thy Saviour King:
  He reigns and triumphs here!"

3 How happy are our ears,
  That hear the joyful sound,
Which kings and prophets waited for,
  And sought, but never found!

4 How blessed are our eyes,
  That see this heavenly light;
Prophets and kings desir'd it long,
  But died without the sight!

65   C. M.

HOW calmly wakes the hallowed dawn!
  How tranquil earth's repose!
Meet emblem of the Sabbath morn
  When, early, Jesus rose.

2 How fair, along the rippling wave,
  The radiant light is cast!
A symbol of the mystic grave
  Through which the Saviour passed.

3 Around this scene of sacred love
  The peace of heaven is shed;
So came the Spirit, like a dove,
  To rest on Jesus' head.

4 Lord, meet us in this path of thine;
  We come thy right to seal;
Move o'er the waters, Dove divine,
  And all thy grace reveal.

66   8s, 6s.

HOW happy are the little flock,
  Who, safe beneath their guardian Rock,
    In all commotions rest!
When war's and tumult's waves run high,
Unmoved above the storm they lie,
    And lodge in Jesus' breast.

2 Such happiness, O Lord, have we,
By mercy gathered in to thee
    Before the floods descend;
And, while the bursting cloud comes down,
We mark the vengeful day begun,
    And calmly wait the end.

3 The plague, and dearth, and din of war,
Our Saviour's swift approach declare,
    And bid our hearts arise;
Earth's basis shook confirms our hope;
Its cities' fall but lifts us up
    To meet thee in the skies.

4 Thy tokens we with joy confess;
The war proclaims thee Prince of Peace;
    The earthquake speaks thy power;
The famine all thy fulness brings;
The plague presents thy healing wings
    And nature's final hour.

5 Whatever ills the world befall
A pledge of endless good we call,
  A sign of Jesus near;
His chariot will not long delay;
We hear the rumbling wheels, and pray,
  "Triumphant Lord, appear!"

67   P. M

HOW happy are they
  Who their Saviour obey,
And have laid up their treasure above!
  Tongue cannot express
  The sweet comfort and peace
Of a soul in its earliest love.

2 That comfort was mine
  When the favour divine
I first found in the blood of the Lamb;
  When my heart it believed,
  What a joy I received,
What a heaven in Jesus' name!

3 'Twas a heaven below
  My Redeemer to know,
And the angels could do nothing more
  Than to fall at his feet,
  And the story repeat,
And the lover of sinners adore.

4 Jesus all the day long
  Was my joy and my song;
O that all his salvation might see!
  He hath loved me, I cried,
  He hath suffered and died,
To redeem even rebels like me.

5 O the rapturous height
  Of that holy delight
Which I felt in the life-giving blood!
  Of my Saviour possessed,
  I was perfectly blest,
As if filled with the fulness of God.

68   C. M.

HOW happy every child of grace,
  Who knows his sins forgiven!
This earth, he cries, is not my place—
  I seek my rest in heaven;
A country far from mortal sight;
  Yet, O, by faith I see
The land of rest, the saint's delight,
  The heaven prepared for me!

2 O, what a blessed hope is ours!
  While here on earth we stay,
We more than taste the heavenly powers,
  And antedate that day;
We feel the resurrection near,
  Our life in Christ concealed,
And with his glorious presence here
  Our earthen vessels filled.

69   P. M.

HOW precious is the name! brethren sing,
    brethren sing,
How precious is the name! brethren sing,
    How precious is the name
    Of Christ, our Paschal Lamb,
Who bore our sin and shame on the tree, on the
Who bore our sin and shame on the tree! [tree!

2 I've given all for Christ, he's my all, he's my
I've given all for Christ, he's my all;   [all;
  I've given all for Christ,
    And my spirit cannot rest,
Unless he's in my breast, reigning there, reign-
      ing there;
Unless he's in my breast reigning there.

3 His easy yoke I'll bear, with delight, with de-
His easy yoke I'll bear, with delight;   [light;
  His easy yoke I'll bear,
    And his cross I will not fear;
His name I will declare, evermore, evermore;
His name I will declare evermore.

70   P. M.

HOW swiftly the years of our pilgrimage fly,
  As days, months and years roll silently by;
Our days are soon numbered, and death sounds
    our knell,
  We scarce know our friends, till we bid them
    farewell.

2 The righteous and unrighteous all move along
  In crowds to the grave, both the old and the
    young;
The good rise to heaven, the bad sink to hell,
  They take on its verge an eternal farewell.

3 Oh God! are mankind hastening on to the
    tomb?
  Must hard-hearted sinners soon meet their
    just doom?
Save! Save! great Redeemer, oh break the sad
    spell:
  Forgive and prepare them to bid earth fare-
    well.

4 To you fellow Christians, I turn with delight,
   The grave cannot harm you, your prospects are bright!
Be faithful and humble, temptations repel,
   You'll soon leave the world with a cheerful farewell.

71   8s.

HOW tedious and tasteless the hours,
   When Jesus no longer I see!
Sweet prospects, sweet birds, and sweet flowers,
   Have all lost their sweetness to me;
The midsummer sun shines but dim,
   The fields strive in vain to look gay;
But when I am happy in him,
   December's as pleasant as May.

2 His name yields the richest perfume,
   And sweeter than music his voice;
His presence disperses my gloom,
   And makes all within me rejoice.
Content with beholding his face,
   My all to his pleasure resigned,
No changes of season or place
   Would make any change in my mind.

3 Dear Lord, if indeed I am thine,
   If thou art my sun and my song,
Say, why do I languish and pine?
   And why are my winters so long?
O, drive these dark clouds from my sky!
   Thy soul-cheering presence restore;
And bid me rejoice in thee nigh;
   Then winter and clouds are no more.

72   7s, 6s.

HOW long, O Lord, our Saviour,
   Wilt thou remain away?
Our hearts are growing weary
   Of thy so long delay;
O, when shall come the moment
   When, brighter far than morn,
The sunshine of thy glory
   Shall on the people dawn?

2 How long, O gracious Master,
   Wilt thou thy household leave?
So long hast thou now tarried,
   Few thy return believe.
Immersed in sloth and folly,
   Thy servants, Lord, we see;
And few of us stand ready
   With joy to welcome thee.

3 How long, O heavenly Bridegroom!
   How long wilt thou delay?
And yet how few are grieving
   That thou dost absent stay!
Thy very bride her portion
   And calling hath forgot,
And seeks for ease and glory
   Where thou, her Lord, art not.

4 O, wake thy slumb'ring virgins!
   Send forth the solemn cry,
Let all thy saints repeat it,
   "The Bridegroom draweth nigh!"
May all our lamps be burning,
   Our loins well girded be,
Each longing heart preparing
   With joy thy face to see.

73
C. M.

"I COME," the great Redeemer cries,
  "To do thy will, O Lord!"
At Jordan's flood, behold, he seals
  The sure prophetic word.

2 "Thus it becomes us to fulfil
  All righteousness," he said;
He spake obedient, and beneath
  The yielding wave was laid.

3 Hark! a glad voice; the Father speaks
  From heaven's exalted height:
"This is my Son, my well-beloved,
  My joy, my chief delight."

74
L. P. M.

I CALL the world's Redeemer mine;
  He lives who died for me, I know,—
Who bought my soul with blood divine:
  Jesus shall re-appear below,—
Stand in that dreadful day unknown,
And fix on earth his heavenly throne.

2 Then the last judgment-day shall come,
  And though the worms this skin devour,
The Judge shall call me from the tomb,
  Shall bid the greedy grave restore,
And raise this individual me,
God in the flesh, my God, to see.

3 In this identic body, I,
  With eyes of flesh refined, restored,
Shall see that self-same Saviour nigh,
  See for myself my smiling Lord;
See with ineffable delight,
Nor faint to bear the glorious sight.

75   C. M.

I KNOW that my Redeemer lives,
   And ever prays for me:
A token of his love he gives,—
   A pledge of liberty.

2 I find him lifting up my head;
   He brings salvation near;
His presence makes me free indeed,
   And he will soon appear.

3 He wills that I should holy be!
   What can withstand his will?
The counsel of his grace in me
   He surely shall fulfil.

4 Jesus, I hang upon thy word;
   I steadfastly believe
Thou wilt return, and claim me, Lord,
   And to thyself receive.

76   P. M.

I'M glad salvation's free,
   And without price or cost;
For had it been for me to buy,
   My soul must have been lost.

CHORUS.
   I'm glad salvation's free—
   I'm glad salvation's free—
   Salvation's free for you and me,
   I'm glad salvation's free.

2 In this cold world below,
   With none to care for me;
A pilgrim lone, without a home,—
   I'm glad salvation's free.

3 Once I was blind and lost,
   Of sin and sorrow full;
But now I'm saved thro' Jesus' blood,—
   I feel it in my soul.

77   P. M.

I'M a pilgrim and I'm a stranger;
   I can tarry, I can tarry but a night;
Do not detain me, for I am going
To where the fountains are ever flowing.

2 There the glory is ever shining;
O, my longing heart, my longing heart is there;
Here in this country so dark and dreary,
I long have wandered forlorn and weary,
   I'm a pilgrim, and I'm a stranger, &c.

3 Farewell, dreary earth, by sin so blighted;
In immortal beauty soon you'll be arrayed;
He who has formed thee, will soon restore thee!
And then thy dread curse shall never more be:
   I'm a pilgrim, and I'm a stranger,   [night.
   Till thy rest shall end the weary pilgrim's

78   P. M.

I'M a lonely trav'ler here,
   Weary, opprest;
But my journey's end is near;
   Soon I shall rest.
Dark and dreary is the way,
   Toiling I've come;
Ask me not with you to stay,—
   Yonder's my home.

2 I'm a weary trav'ler here,
 I must go on;
For my journey's end is near;
 I must be gone.
Brighter joys than earth can give
 Win me away;
Pleasures that forever live,—
 I cannot stay.

3 I'm a trav'ler to a land
 Where all is fair;
Where is seen no broken band;
 All, all are there.
Where no tear shall ever fall,
 Nor heart be sad;
Where the glory is for all,
 And all are glad.

79   L. M.

I'M not ashamed to own my Lord,
 Who lives by angels now adored;
That Jesus who once died for me,
Who bore my sins in agony.

2 I'm not ashamed to own his laws,
Nor to defend his noble cause;
The way he's gone is lined with blood;
O may I tread the steps he trod!

3 I'm not ashamed his name to bear,
With those who his disciples were;
Christian, sweet name! its worth I view,
O may I wear the nature too!

4 I'm not ashamed to bear my cross,
For which I count all things but dross;

Whate'er I'm bid to do or say,
When Christ commands, I will obey.

5 I'm not ashamed to be despised
By those who ne'er religion prized;
Nor will I prove to Christ untrue,
For all that men can say or do.

6 This world's vain honors will I shun,
The narrow way to life I'll run;
That this at last my boast may be,
My Saviour's not ashamed of me.

80   C. M.

IN hope of an immortal crown
   I now the cross sustain,
And gladly wander up and down,
   And smile at toil and pain:
I suffer on my threescore years,
   Till my Deliv'rer come,
And wipe away his servant's tears,
   And take his exile home.

2 O what hath Jesus bought for me!
   Before my ravish'd eyes
Rivers of life divine I see,
   And trees of Paradise:
I see the blessed saints in light
   Who taste the pleasures there;
They all are robed in spotless white,
   And conqu'ring palms they bear.

3 O what are all my suff'rings here,
   If, Lord, thou count me meet
With that enraptured host t' appear,
   And worship at thy feet!

Give joy or grief, give ease or pain,
  Take life or friends away,
But let me find them all again
  In that eternal day.

81   S. M.

IN expectation sweet,
  We'll wait, and sing, and pray,
Till Christ's triumphal car we meet,
  And see an endless day.

2 He comes, the Conq'ror comes;
  Death falls beneath his sword;
The joyful pris'ners burst the tombs,
  And rise to meet their Lord.

82   8s.

I NOW am so blessed with his love,
  I covet not earth's greatest store;
He visits me oft from above—
  I have him, I want nothing more:
Resigned to his pleasure I'd live,
  Till time's latest circle shall roll,
His utmost salvation receive,
  For, oh! he spoke peace to my soul.

2 Ye angels who wait while I sing,
  And patiently hear my glad song,
Come, bear me to Jesus, my King,
  To join with the heavenly throng.
'Tis there I'll eternally feast
  On joys that enrapture the whole;
All heaven would welcome the guest,
  Since Jesus spoke peace to my soul.

8

83   L. M.

I THIRST, thou wounded Lamb of God,
To wash me in thy cleansing blood;
To dwell within thy wounds; then pain
Is sweet, and life or death is gain.

2 Take my poor heart, and let it be
Forever closed to all but thee:
Seal thou my breast, and let me wear
That pledge of love forever there.

3 How can it be, thou heavenly King,
That thou shouldst us to glory bring;
Make slaves the partners of thy throne,
Deck'd with a never-fading crown?

4 Hence our hearts melt, our eyes o'erflow,
Our words are lost, nor will we know,
Nor will we think of aught beside,—
My Lord, my Love, is crucified.

84   C. M.

I LOVE to steal awhile away
From every cumb'ring care,
And spend the hours of setting day
In humble, grateful prayer.

2 I love in solitude to shed
The penitential tear,
And all his promises to plead
Where none but God can hear.

3 I love to think on mercies past,
And future good implore,—
And all my cares and sorrows cast
On Him whom I adore.

85   7s.

IN the sun, and moon, and stars,
  Signs and wonders there shall be;
Earth shall quake with inward wars,
  Nations with perplexity.

2 Soon shall ocean's hoary deep,
  Tossed with stronger tempests rise;
Darker storms the mountains sweep,
  Fiercer lightnings rend the skies.

3 Evil thoughts shall shake the proud,
  Racking doubt and restless fear;
And, amid the thunder-cloud,
  Shall the Judge of men appear.

4 But, though from that awful face
  Heaven shall fade and earth shall fly,
Fear not ye, his chosen race;
  Your redemption draweth nigh.

86   H. M.

JESUS, accept the praise
  That to thy Name belongs;
Matter of all our lays,
  Subject of all our songs;
Through thee we now together came,
And part exulting in thy Name.

2 In flesh we part awhile,
  But still in spirit joined,
T' embrace the happy toil
  Thou hast to each assign'd;
And while we do thy blessed will,
We bear our heaven about us still.

3 O let us thus go on
    In all thy pleasant ways,
And, arm'd with patience, run
    With joy the' appointed race:
Keep us and every seeking soul,
Till all attain the heavenly goal.

87   P. M.
JESUS died on Calv'ry's mountain,
        Long time ago,
And salvation's rolling fountain
        Now freely flows.

2 Once his voice in tones of pity
        Melted in wo,
And he wept o'er Judah's city
        Long time ago.

3 On his head the dews of midnight
        Fell, long ago;
Now a crown of dazzling sunlight
        Sits on his brow.

4 Jesus died, yet lives forever,
        No more to die;
Bleeding Jesus, blessed Saviour,
        Now sits on high.

5 Now in heaven he's interceding
        For dying men,
Soon he'll finish all his pleading,
        And come again.

6 Budding fig-trees tell that summer
        Dawns o'er the land;
Signs portend that Jesus' coming
        Is near at hand.

7 When he comes, a voice from heaven
    Shall pierce the tomb:
"Come, ye blessed of my Father,
    Children, come home."

88   P. M.

JESUS, faithful to his word,
  Shall with a shout descend;
All heaven's host their glorious Lord
  Shall joyfully attend.
Christ shall come with dreadful noise,
  Lightnings swift and thunders loud;
With the great archangel's voice,
  And with the trump of God.

2 First the dead in Christ shall rise;
  Then we that yet remain
Shall be caught up to the skies,
  And see our Lord again.
We shall meet him in the air,
  All caught up to heaven shall be;
Find, and love, and praise him there,
  From death forever free.

89   C. M.

JESUS hath died that I might live,
  Might live to God alone;
In him eternal life receive,
  And be in spirit one.

2 Saviour, I thank thee for the grace,
  The gift unspeakable;
And wait with arms of faith t' embrace,
  And all thy love to feel.

3 My soul breaks out in strong desire
　　The perfect bliss to prove;
My longing heart is all on fire
　　To be dissolved in love.

4 Give me thyself: from every boast,
　　From every wish set free;
Let all I am in thee be lost,
　　But give thyself to me.

90　　　　　　　　　　　　　　8s.

JESUS, I my cross have taken,
　　All to leave, and follow thee:
Naked, poor, despised, forsaken,
　　Thou, from hence, my all shalt be;
Perish every fond ambition,
　　All I've sought, or hoped, or known!
Yet how rich is my condition,
　　God and heaven are still my own!

2 Let the world despise and leave me;
　　They have left my Saviour, too;
Human hearts and looks deceive me,
　　Thou art not, like them, untrue;
O, while thou dost smile upon me,
　　God of wisdom, love, and might!
Foes may hate, and friends disown me,
　　Show thy face, and all is bright.

91　　　　　　　　　　　　　　7s.

JESUS, lover of my soul!
　　Let me to thy bosom fly,
While the billows near me roll,
　　While the tempest still is high;

Hide me, O my Saviour, hide
   Till the storm of life be past!
Safe into the haven guide;
   O! receive my soul at last.

2 Other refuge have I none,—
   Hangs my helpless soul on thee:
Leave, ah! leave me not alone;
   Still support and comfort me:
All my trust on thee is stayed;
   All my help from thee I bring:
Cover my defenceless head
   With the shadow of thy wing.

92   L. M.

JESUS, my all, to heaven is gone,
   He whom I fix my hopes upon;
His track I see, and I'll pursue
The narrow way, till him I view.

2 The way the holy prophets went,
The road that leads from banishment,
The King's highway of holiness,
I'll go, for all his paths are peace.

3 This is the way I long have sought,
And mourned because I found it not;
My grief, my burden long has been
Because I could not cease from sin.

4 The more I strove against its power,
I sinned and stumbled but the more;
Till late I heard my Saviour say,
"Come hither, soul: I am the way."

5 Lo, glad I come; and thou, blest Lamb,
Wilt take me to thee as I am;

Nothing but sin I thee can give,
Nothing but love shall I receive.

6 Then will I tell to sinners round
What a dear Saviour I have found;
I'll point to thy redeeming blood,
And say, "Behold the way to God."

93 P. M.

JESUS our Saviour says, I will appear;
    Have you faith?
My trumpet is sounding majestic and clear;
    Have you faith?
  The faithful alone I come to see,
  And they shall live and reign with me:
Only have faith! only have faith! only have faith!

2 Prophets have spoken, their words are ful-
    Have you faith?   [filled;
My word is established, your anguish is stilled;
    Have you faith?
  The plan of salvation the faith's eye will see,
  And live forever and reign with me;
Only have faith! only have faith! only have faith!

3 Though I should tarry be not dismayed;
    Have you faith?
The judgment is coming o'er all, I have said;
    Have you faith?
  The doubt to the bondage, the faith to the
  To live forever and reign with me;   [free,
Only have faith! only have faith! only have faith!

94 C. M.

JESUS, the Name high over all,
  In hell, or earth, or sky:

Angels and men before it fall,
 And devils fear and fly.

2 Jesus, the Name to sinners dear,—
 The Name to sinners given;
It scatters all their guilty fear;
 It turns their hell to heaven.

3 Jesus the pris'ner's fetters breaks,
 And bruises Satan's head;
Power into strengthless souls he speaks,
 And life into the dead.

4 O that the world might taste and see
 The riches of his grace;
The arms of love that compass me,
 Would all mankind embrace.

5 His only righteousness I show,—
 His saving truth proclaim:
'Tis all my business here below,
 To cry,—Behold the Lamb!

6 Happy, if with my latest breath
 I may but gasp his name;
Preach him to all, and cry in death,
 Behold, behold the Lamb!

95   C. M.

JESUS, thine all-victorious love
 Shed in my heart abroad:
Then shall my feet no longer rove,
 Rooted and fixed in God.

2 O that in me the sacred fire
 Might now begin to glow;
Burn up the dross of base desire,
 And make the mountains flow.

3 O that it now from heaven might fall,
  And all my sins consume:
Come, Holy Ghost, for thee I call;
  Spirit of burning, come.

4 Refining fire, go through my heart;
  Illuminate my soul;
Scatter thy life through every part,
  And sanctify the whole.

96   L. M.

JESUS shall reign where'er the sun
  Does his successive journeys run;
His kingdom spread from shore to shore,
Till moons shall wax and wane no more.

2 To him shall endless prayer be made,
And endless praises crown his head;
His Name like sweet perfume shall rise
With every morning sacrifice.

3 People and realms of every tongue
Dwell on his love with sweetest song,
And infant voices shall proclaim
Their early blessings on his Name.

97   P. M.

JUST as thou art,—without one trace
  Of love, or joy, or inward grace,
Or meetness for the heavenly place,
    O guilty sinner, come!

2 Thy sins I bore on Calvary's tree;
The stripes thy due were laid on me,
That peace and pardon might be free,—
    O wretched sinner, come!

3 Come, leave thy burden at the cross;
Count all thy gains but empty dross:
My grace repays all earthly loss,—
    O needy sinner, come!

4 Come, hither bring thy boding fears,
Thy aching heart, thy bursting tears;
'Tis mercy's voice salutes thine ears,—
    O trembling sinner, come!

98   P. M.

JUST as I am, without one plea
  But that thy blood was shed for me,
And that thou bidd'st me come to thee,
    O Lamb of God, I come!

2 Just as I am, and waiting not
To rid my soul of one dark blot,
To thee, whose blood can cleanse each spot,
    O Lamb of God, I come!

3 Just as I am, though tossed about
With many a conflict, many a doubt,
With fears within and wars without,
    O Lamb of God, I come!

4 Just as I am, poor, wretched, blind,
Sight, riches, healing of the mind,
Yea, all I need, in thee to find,
    O Lamb of God, I come!

99   C. M.

JERUSALEM, my happy home,
  O, how I long for thee!
When will my sorrows have an end?
  Thy joys when shall I see?

2 Thy walls are all of precious stones,
    Most glorious to behold:
Thy gates are richly set with pearl,
    Thy streets are paved with gold.

3 Thy gardens and thy pleasant walks
    My study long have been;
Such dazzling views by human sight
    Have never yet been seen.

4 If such thy holy city, Lord,
    Why should we linger here,
Still cleaving to this vile abode,
    Nor wish thee to appear?

100 L. M.

JESUS, thy blood and righteousness,
    My beauty are, my glorious dress:
'Midst flaming worlds, in these array'd,
With joy shall I lift up my head.

2 Bold shall I stand in thy great day,
For who aught to my charge shall lay?
Fully absolved through these I am,—
From sin and fear, from guilt and shame.

3 The holy, meek, unspotted Lamb,
Who from the Father's bosom came,—
Who died for me, e'en me, t' atone,—
Now for my Lord and God I own.

4 Lord, I believe thy precious blood,—
Which, at the mercy-seat of God,
Forever doth for sinners plead,—
For me, e'en for my soul, was shed.

5 Lord, I believe were sinners more
Than sands upon the ocean shore,
Thou hast for all a ransom paid,
For all a full atonement made.

101   L. M.

JESUS, thou everlasting King,
Accept the tribute which we bring;
Accept thy well-deserved renown,
And wear our praises as thy crown.

2 Let every act of worship be
Like our espousals, Lord, to thee:
Like the blest hour, when from above
We first received the pledge of love.

3 The gladness of that happy day,
O may it ever, ever stay:
Nor let our faith forsake its hold,
Nor hope decline, nor love grow cold.

4 Let every moment, as it flies,
Increase thy praise, improve our joys,
Till we are raised to sing thy Name,
At the great supper of the Lamb.

102   C. M.

LET every mortal ear attend,
And every heart rejoice;
The trumpet of the gospel sounds
With an inviting voice.

2 Ho! all ye hungry, starving souls,
That feed upon the wind,
And vainly strive with earthly toys
To fill an empty mind:—

3 Eternal Wisdom hath prepared
A soul-reviving feast,
And bids your longing appetites
The rich provision taste.

4 Ho! ye that pant for living streams,
And pine away and die,
Here you may quench your raging thirst
From springs that never dry.

5 Rivers of love and mercy here
In a rich ocean join;
Salvation in abundance flows,
Like floods of milk and wine.

6 The happy gates of gospel grace
Stand open night and day:
Lord, we are come to seek supplies,
And drive our wants away.

103   C. M.

LET Zion's watchmen all awake,
And take th' alarm they give:
Now let them from the mouth of God
Their awful charge receive.

2 'Tis not a cause of small import
The pastor's care demands;
It occupies the Saviour's heart,
Employs angelic bands.

3 They watch for souls, for which the Lord
Did heavenly bliss forego;
For souls which by his grace may live,
Or perish in their wo.

4 May they that Jesus whom they preach
 Their own Redeemer see;
And watch thou daily for their souls,
 That they may watch for thee.

104 P. M.

LIFT up your heads, Immanuel's friends,
 And taste the pleasure Jesus sends;
Let nothing cause you to delay,
But hasten on the good old way.

CHORUS.

And I'll sing hallelujah,
And glory be to God on high;
And I'll sing hallelujah,
There's glory beaming through the sky.

2. Our conflicts here though great they be,
Shall not prevent our victory;
If we but watch, and strive, and pray,
Like soldiers in the good old way.

3. Oh good old way! how sweet thou art,
May none of us from thee depart;
But may our actions always say,
We're marching in the good old way.

105 P. M.

LOW down in this beautiful valley,
 Where love crowns the meek and the lowly,
Where no storms of envy or folly,
 May roll on their billows in vain.

This low vale is far from contention,
Where no soul can dream of dissension,
No dark wiles of evil invention,
  Can find out this region of peace.

2 The low soul in humble subjection,
Shall here find unshaken protection,
And soft gales of cheering reflection,
  A mind soothed from sorrow and pain.
O there, there, the Lord will deliver,
And souls drink of that beautiful river,
Where peace flows for ever and ever,
  Where love and joy will ever increase.

3 There, there, in yonder bright glory,
We'll sing, shout, and tell the glad story,
When we've passed cold Jordan quite over,
  We'll sing hallelujah to God and the Lamb.
Yes, there, there, the Lord will deliver,
And souls drink of that beautiful river,
Where peace flows for ever and ever,
  Where love and joy will ever increase.

106 8s. 7s. 4s.

LO, he comes, with clouds descending,
  Once for favored sinners slain!
Thousand, thousand saints attending,
  Swell the triumph of his train.
    Hallelujah!
  Jesus comes on earth to reign!

2 When the solemn trump has sounded,
  Heaven and earth shall flee away,
All who hate him must, confounded,
  Hear the summons of that day:
    Come to judgment!
  Come to judgment, come away!

3 Yea, amen; let all adore thee,
   High on thine eternal throne!
Saviour, take the power and glory,
   Make thy righteous sentence known.
     O come quickly—
   Claim the kingdom for thine own!

107   8s. 7s. 4s.

LOOK, ye saints, the sight is glorious!
   See the "Man of Sorrows" now;
From the fight returned victorious,
   Every knee to him shall bow.
     Crown him, crown him!
   Crowns become the Victor's brow!

2 Crown the Saviour, angels crown him!
   Rich the trophies Jesus brings;
In the seat of power enthrone him,
   While the vault of heaven rings.
     Crown him, crown him!
   Crown the Saviour "King of kings!"

108   C. M.

LO, what a glorious sight appears
   To our believing eyes!
The earth and seas are passed away,
   And the old rolling skies!

2 From the third heaven, where God resides,
   That holy, happy place,
The New Jerusalem comes down,
   Adorned with shining grace.

3 Attending angels shout for joy,
   And the bright armies sing:

"Mortals, behold the sacred seat
    Of your descending King!

4 The God of glory down to men
    Removes his blest abode;
Men are the objects of his love,
    And he their gracious God.

5 His own soft hand shall wipe the tears
    From every weeping eye;
And pains, and groans, and griefs, and fears,
    And death itself, shall die."

6 How bright the vision! O, how long
    Shall this glad hour delay!
Fly swifter round, ye wheels of time,
    And bring the welcome day!

109   C. M.

LORD, in the morning thou shalt hear
    My voice ascending high;
To thee will I direct my prayer;
    To thee lift up mine eye:

2 Up to the hills where Christ is gone
    To plead for all his saints,
Presenting at his Father's throne
    Our songs and our complaints.

3 Thou art a God before whose sight
    The wicked shall not stand;
Sinners shall ne'er be thy delight,
    Nor dwell at thy right hand.

4 But to thy house will I resort,
    To taste thy mercies there;
I will frequent thy holy court,
    And worship in thy fear.

110   L. M.

LORD, let thy presence now attend
Him whom we to thy grace commend;
Nor let him as a pilgrim rove,
Without the conduct of thy love.

2 Thy promise stands upon record
To be with those who preach thy word;
Be with him, Lord, the work is thine;
Support him with thy strength divine.

3 Inflame his zeal, enlarge his heart,
Courage and utterance impart;
His love be ardent, pure his aim,
The great salvation be his theme.

4 While thronging multitudes around
Hear from his lips the joyful sound,
Thy power impart, thy gospel bless,
And crown his labors with success.

5 O may his eyes with joy behold
Thy grace, as in the days of old!
May sinners tremble at thy word,
Believe and turn unto the Lord.

111   [Peculiar.] 8s, 7s.

MARK that pilgrim lowly bending
At the shrine of prayer, ascending
Praise and sighs together blending
From his lips in mournful strain;
Glowing with sincere contrition,
And with childlike, blest submission,
Ever riseth this petition:
"Jesus, come, O come to reign!"

2 List again: the low earth sigheth,
And the blood of martyrs crieth
From its bosom, where there lieth
　Millions upon millions slain;
"Lord, how long," ere, thy word given,
All the wicked shall be driven
From the earth by bolts of heaven?
　"Jesus, come, O come to reign!"

3 Kingdoms now are reeling, falling,
Nations lie in wo appalling,
On their sages vainly calling
　All these wonders to explain;
While the slain around are lying,
God's own little flock are sighing,
And in secret places crying,
　"Jesus, come, O come to reign!"

112 P. M.

MUST Simon bear his cross alone,
　And all the world go free?
No; there's a cross for every one,
　And there's a cross for me.
Yes, there's a cross on Calvary,
Through which by faith the crown I see;
　To me 'tis pardon bringing;
　　O, that's the cross for me!

2 How faithful does the Saviour prove
　To those who serve him here!
They now may taste his perfect love,
　And joy to hail him near.
Yes, perfect love will dry the tear,
And cast out all tormenting fear,
　Which round my heart is clinging;
　　O, that's the love for me!

3 We'll bear the consecrated cross,
   Till from the cross we're free,
And then go home to wear the crown,
   For there's a crown for me.
Yes, there's a crown in heaven above,
The purchase of my Saviour's love,
   For me at His appearing;
     O, that's the crown for me!

113   C. M.

MY drowsy powers, why sleep ye so?
   Awake, my sluggish soul;
Nothing has half thy work to do,
   Yet nothing's half so dull.

2 Go to the ants: for one poor grain
   See how they toil and strive!
Yet we, who have a heaven t' obtain,
   How negligent we live!

3 We, for whose sake all nature stands,
   And stars their courses move;
We, for whose guard the angel bands
   Come flying from above;

4 We, for whom God the Son came down,
   And labored for our good;
How careless to secure that crown
   He purchased with His blood!

114   8s, 7s.

MY days are gliding swiftly by,
   And I, a pilgrim stranger,
Would not detain them as they fly,
   Those hours of toil and danger.

2 We'll gird our loins, my brethren dear,
  Our heavenly home discerning;
Our absent Lord has left us word,
  Let every lamp be burning.

3 Should coming days be cold and dark,
  We need not cease our singing;
That perfect rest naught can molest,
  Where golden harps are ringing.

4 Let sorrow's rudest tempest blow,
  Each chord on earth to sever;
Our King says come, and there's our home,
  Forever, O forever!

CHORUS.

For O! we stand on Jordan's strand,
  Our friends are passing over.
And just before, the shining shore
  We may almost discover.

115 P. M.

MY faith looks up to thee,
  Thou Lamb of Calvary,
    Saviour divine!
Now hear me while I pray,
Take all my guilt away,
O let me from this day
  Be wholly thine.

2 May thy rich grace impart
Strength to my fainting heart;
  My zeal inspire:
As thou hast died for me,
O may my love to thee,
Pure, warm, and changeless be,
  A living fire.

116   P. M.

MY soul's full of glory, inspiring my tongue:
  Could I meet with angels I'd sing them a song;
I'd sing of my Jesus, and tell of his charms,
And beg them to bear me to his loving arms.

2 Methinks they're descending to hear what I sing; [king:
Well pleased to hear mortals while praising their
O angels! O angels! my soul's in a flame,
I faint in sweet raptures at Jesus' name.

3 O Jesus! O Jesus! thou balm of my soul,
'Twas thou, my dear Jesus, that made my heart whole:
Oh! bring me to view thee, thou glorious king;
In regions of glory thy praises to sing.

117   C. M.

MORTALS, awake, with angels join,
  And chant the solemn lay;
Joy, love, and gratitude combine,
  To hail th' auspicious day.

2 In heaven the rapt'rous song began,
  And sweet seraphic fire
Through all the shining legions ran,
  And strung and tuned the lyre.

3 Swift through the vast expanse it flew,
  And loud the echo roll'd;
The theme, the song, the joy, was new,—
  'Twas more than heaven could hold.

4 Down through the portals of the sky
    Th' impetuous torrent ran;
And angels flew, with eager joy,
    To bear the news to man.

5 With joy the chorus we repeat,—
    Glory to God on high!
Good-will and peace are now complete—
    Jesus was born to die.

6 Hail, Prince of life, forever hail!
    Redeemer, Brother, Friend!
Though earth, and time, and life shall fail,
    Thy praise shall never end.

118   C. M.

MY soul is happy when I hear
    The Saviour is so nigh:
I long to see his sign appear
    Upon the op'ning sky.

2 I love to wait, and watch, and pray,
    And trust his living word,
And feel the coming of that day
    No longer is deferred.

3 I do rejoice that life was given
    In these last days to me,
That deathless I may rise to heaven,
    And my Redeemer see.

4 Then, waiting brethren, let us sing;
    He will not tarry long;
And fill with love the hours that bring
    The glory of our song.

5 Yes, he will come, no longer fear,
   Though earth and hell assail;
His word attests the moment near,
   And that can never fail.

119   C. M.

NOW from the altar of our hearts
   Let flames of love arise;
Assist us, Lord, to offer up
   Our evening sacrifice.

2 Minutes and mercies multiplied
   Have made up all this day;
Minutes came quick, but mercies were
   More swift, more free than they.

3 New time, new favors, and new joys,
   Do a new song require;
Till we shall praise thee as we would,
   Accept our hearts' desire.

4 In every joy that crowns my days,
   In every pain I bear,
My heart shall find delight in praise,
   Or seek relief in prayer.

120   8s, 6s.

O, COULD we speak the matchless worth,
   O, could we sound the glories forth,
      Which in our Saviour shine?
We'd soar and touch the heavenly strings,
And vie with Gabriel, while he sings,
   In notes almost divine.

2 We'd sing the characters he bears,
And all the forms of love he wears,
    Exalted on his throne;
In loftiest songs of sweetest praise
We would to everlasting days
    Make all his glories known.

121   C. M.

O FOR a faith that will not shrink,
    Though pressed by many a foe;
That will not tremble on the brink
    Of poverty or wo;

2 That will not murmur nor complain
    Beneath the chast'ning rod;
But in the hour of grief or pain
    Can lean upon its God.

3 A faith that shines more bright and clear
    When tempests rage without;
That when in danger knows no fear,
    In darkness feels no doubt.

4 Lord, give me such a faith as this,
    And then, whate'er may come,
I'll taste e'en here the hallowed bliss
    Of an eternal home.

122   C. M.

O FOR a heart to praise my God;
    A heart from sin set free;
A heart that's sprinkled with the blood
    So freely shed for me;

2 An humble, lowly, contrite heart,
    Believing, true, and clean,

    Which neither life nor death can part
      From him that dwells within;

3 A heart in every thought renewed,
    And filled with love divine;
  Perfect, and right, and pure, and good;
    A copy, Lord, of thine!

4 Thy nature, gracious Lord, impart;
    Come quickly from above;
  Write thy new name upon my heart,
    Thy new best name of love.

123   C. M.

O FOR a thousand tongues to sing
    My great Redeemer's praise,—
  The glories of my God and King,
    The triumphs of His grace!

2 My gracious Master and my God,
    Assist me to proclaim,
  To spread through all the earth abroad
    The honors of thy name.

3 Jesus! the name that calms our fears,
    That bids our sorrows cease;
  'Tis music in the sinner's ears;
    'Tis life, and health, and peace,

4 Look unto him, ye nations; own
    Your God, ye fallen race;
  Look, and be saved through faith alone,
    Be justified by grace.

124　　　　　　　　　　　　　　L. M.

O HAPPY day that fixed my choice
  On thee, my Saviour and my God!
Well may this glowing heart rejoice,
  And tell its raptures all abroad.
    Happy day, happy day,
    When Jesus washed my sins away;
    He taught me how to watch and pray,
    And live rejoicing every day.

2 Oh! happy bond that seals my vows
  To him who merits all my love,
Let cheerful anthems fill his house,
  While to that sacred shrine I move.

3 'Tis done, the great transaction's done:
  I am my Lord's, and he is mine;
He drew me, and I followed on,
  Charmed to confess the voice divine.

125　　　　　　　　　　　　　　H. M.

O HAPPY, happy day,
  That calls thy exiles home;
The heavens shall pass away,
  The earth receive its doom:
Earth we shall view, and heaven, destroy'd,
And shout above the fiery void.

2 According to his word,
  His oath, to sinners given,
We look to see restored
  The ruin'd earth and heaven;
In a world his truth to prove,
A world of righteousness and love.

3 Then let us wait the sound
 That shall our souls release,
And labor to be found
 Of Him in spotless peace:
In perfect holiness renew'd,
Adorn'd with Christ, and meet for God.

126   C. M.

O JOYFUL sound of gospel grace,
 Christ shall in me appear;
I, even I, shall see his face,—
 I shall be holy here.

2 The glorious crown of righteousness
 To me reach'd out I view:
Conqu'ror through him, I soon shall seize,
 And wear it as my due.

3 The promised land, from Pisgah's top,
 I now exult to see:
My hope is full, (O glorious hope!)
 Of immortality.

4 With me, I know, I feel, thou art;
 But this cannot suffice,
Unless thou plantest in my heart
 A constant paradise.

5 My earth thou wat'rest from on high,
 But make it all a pool:
Spring up, O Well, I ever cry;
 Spring up within my soul.

127   8s, 6s.

O LOVE divine, how sweet thou art!
 When shall I find my willing heart
  All taken up by thee?

I thirst, I faint, I die to prove
The greatness of redeeming love,—
   The love of Christ to me.

2 Stronger his love than death or hell:
Its riches are unsearchable:
   The first-born sons of light
Desire in vain its depths to see;
They cannot reach the mystery,
   The length, the breadth, the height.

128   C. M.

ON Jordan's stormy banks I stand,
   And cast a wishful eye
To Canaan's fair and happy land,
   Where my possessions lie.

2 O, the transporting, rapt'rous scene
   That rises to my sight!
Sweet fields arrayed in living green,
   And rivers of delight.

3 There gen'rous fruits, that never fail,
   On trees immortal grow;
There rock, and hill, and brook, and vale,
   With milk and honey flow.

4 O'er all those wide-extended plains
   Shines one eternal day;
There God the Son forever reigns,
   And scatters night away.

5 No chilling winds, nor pois'nous breath
   Can reach that healthful shore;
Sickness and sorrow, pain and death,
   Are felt and feared no more.

129   P. M.

ON the high cliffs of Jordan with pleasure I stand,
And view in perspective the fair promised land:
The land where the ransomed with singing shall come,
And enter the kingdom prepared as their home.

2 There rivers most graceful eternally glide,
And groves rich with verdure grow up by their side;
There spirits made perfect forever become
Immortal and beauteous, in glory, their home.

3 'Tis there all the nations redeemed by the Lamb
In circles most lovely his praises proclaim;
Through tempests, and sorrow, and perils they come,
To enter those mansions prepared as their home.

4 Those pleasures of glory, O, when shall I share,
And crowns of celestial felicity wear;
And range o'er those landscapes, exempt from a sigh;
The home of our fathers, now specially nigh!

130   L. M.

ON Tabor's top the Saviour stands;
  His altered face resplendent shines,
And while he elevates his hands,
  Lo, glory marks its gentle lines!

2 Two heavenly forms descend to wait
  Upon their suffering Prince below;
But while they worship at his feet,
  They talk of fast approaching wo.

3 Amid the lustre of the scene.
   To Calvary he turns his eyes.
And, with submission all serene.
   He marks the future tempest rise.

4 Then let us climb the mount of prayer.
   Where all his beaming glories shine.
And, gazing on his brightness there.
   Our woes forget in joys divine.

131   L. M.

O THOU, whom all thy saints adore.
   We now with all thy saints agree,
And bow our inmost souls before
   Thy glorious, awful Majesty.

2 We come, great God, to seek thy face.
   And for thy loving-kindness wait;
And O, how dreadful is this place!
   'Tis God's own house, 'tis heaven's gate.

3 Tremble, our hearts, to find thee nigh;
   To thee our trembling hearts aspire:
And lo! we see descend from high
   The pillar and the flame of fire.

4 Still let it on th' assembly stay,
   And all the house with glory fill:
To Canaan's bounds point out the way,
   And lead us to thy holy hill.

5 There let us all with Jesus stand,
   And join the gen'ral Church above,
And take our seats at thy right hand,
   And sing thine everlasting love.

132   L. M.

O THAT my load of sin were gone;
  O that I could at last submit
At Jesus' feet to lay it down—
  To lay my soul at Jesus' feet.

2 Rest for my soul I long to find:
  Saviour of all, if mine thou art,
Give me thy meek and lowly mind,
  And stamp thine image on my heart.

3 Break off the yoke of inbred sin,
  And fully set my spirit free;
I cannot rest till pure within,—
  Till I am wholly lost in thee.

4 Fain would I learn of thee, my God:
  Thy light and easy burden prove;
The cross all stain'd with hallow'd blood,
  The labor of thy dying love.

133   8s. 7s.

O THOU God of my salvation,
  My Redeemer from all sin;
Mov'd by thy divine compassion,
  Who hast died my heart to win,
I will praise thee, I will praise thee,
  Where shall I thy praise begin?

2 Though unseen, I love the Saviour;
  He hath brought salvation near;
Manifests his pard'ning favor;
  And when Jesus doth appear,
Soul and body, soul and body,
  Shall his glorious image bear.

3 While the angel choirs are crying,
  Glory to the Great I AM!
I with them will still be vying,
  Glory! glory to the Lamb!
O how precious, O how precious,
  Is the sound of Jesus' name!

134 H. M.

O THE amazing change!
  A world created new!
My thoughts with transport range,
  The lovely scene to view:
Thee, Lord divine, in all I trace;
The work is thine—thine be the praise.

2 Where pointed brambles grew,
  Entwined with horrid thorn,
Gay flowers, forever new,
  The painted fields adorn;
The lily there, and blushing rose,
In union fair their sweets disclose.

3 The tyrants of the plain
  Their savage chase give o'er;
No more they rend the slain,
  They thirst for blood no more;
But infant hands fierce tigers lead,
And lions with the oxen feed.

4 O, when, almighty Lord,
  Shall these glad scenes arise
To verify thy word,
  And bless our wond'ring eyes;
That earth, with all her tongues, may raise
United songs of ardent praise?

135   C. M.

O 'TIS delight without alloy,
  Jesus, to hear thy name:
My spirit leaps with inward joy;
  I feel the sacred flame.

2 My passions hold a pleasing reign,
  When love inspires my breast,—
Love, the divinest of the train,
  The sov'reign of the rest.

3 This is the grace must live and sing,
  When faith and hope shall cease,
And sound from every joyful string
  Through all the realms of bliss.

4 Swift I ascend the heavenly place,
  And hasten to my home;
I leap to meet thy kind embrace;
  I come, O Lord, I come.

5 Sink down, ye separating hills;
  Let sin and death remove;
'Tis love that drives my chariot wheels,
  And death must yield to love.

136   P. M.

OUR bondage it will end by and by, when he comes;
Our bondage it will end when he comes;
  And, from Egypt's yoke set free,
  Hail the glorious jubilee;
And to glory we'll return by and by, when he [comes;
And to glory we'll return when he comes.

2 Our Deliverer he will come, by and by;
  And our sorrows have an end
    When our Saviour shall descend, [comes;
  And glory crown the day, by and by, when he
  And glory crown the day when he comes.

3 Though our enemies are strong, we'll go on,
  Though our hearts do sometimes fear;
    Lo, Israel's God is near, [go on.
  And the fiery pillar moves; we'll go on, we'll
  And the fiery pillar moves; we'll go on.

137   P. M.

OUR Father, who in heaven art,
  Hallowed be thy name;
Thy kingdom come; thy will be done
  In heaven and earth the same.
    Come, my Saviour! O, my Saviour!
    Come and bless thy people now,
    While at thy feet we humbly bow;
    O come and save us now!
    Then will we sing, our suff'rings o'er.
    And praise thee evermore.

2 Give us this day our daily bread;
    Our trespasses forgive;
  As we forgive our fellow-men,
    May we thy grace receive.

3 And in temptation leave us not;
    From evil us defend:
  For thine, O Lord, the kingdom is,
    Forever, without end.

4 Thine is the power, O Lord, to bring
    The kingdom down to men;
  Thine is the glory evermore,
    And kingdom without end.

5 In that glad day shall all thy saints
   A joyful tribute bring.
Of praise and power, of joy and song,
   To their exalted King.

138   7s. 6s.

O WHEN shall I see Jesus,
   And in his kingdom dwell;
Partake in rest eternal,
   Its songs triumphant swell?
When shall I be delivered
   From this vain world of sin,
And, with my blessed Jesus,
   Drink endless pleasures in?

2 Our eyes shall then, with rapture,
   The Saviour's face behold;
Our feet, no more diverted,
   Shall walk the streets of gold;
Our ears shall hear with transport
   The hosts celestial sing;
Our tongues shall chant the glory
   Of our immortal King.

139   P. M.

O SINNER, come, without delay,
   And seek a home in glory!
The Lord is calling you to-day,
   He pleads for you in glory.
     O glory! O glory!
     There's power in Jesus' dying love
     To bring you home to glory.

2 O turn and live, to you he cries,
   And you shall share my glory!
But, if my mercy you despise,
   You cannot see my glory.

3 Repent, and give him now your heart;
   He is the Lord of glory;
Confess his name, secure a part
   When he shall come in glory.

4 Now is your time; no more delay,
   For soon he'll come in glory;
When, shut without, in vain you'll pray;
   You've lost all hope of glory.

5 O do not madly slight his grace,
   And lose the crown of glory;
But now, before you leave this place,
   Begin the race for glory.

140   7s.

PALMS of glory, raiment bright,
   Crowns that never fade away,
Gird and deck the saints in light;
   Priests, and kings, and conquerors, they.

2 Yet the conquerors bring their palms
   To the Lamb amid the throne;
And proclaim, in joyful psalms,
   Victory through his cross alone.

3 Kings for harps their crowns resign,
   Crying, as they strike the chords—
"Take the kingdom; it is thine,
   King of kings, and Lord of lords."

141   C. M.

PLUNGED in a gulf of dark despair,
    We wretched sinners lay,
Without one cheerful beam of hope,
    Or spark of glimm'ring day.

2 With pitying eyes, the Prince of grace
    Beheld our helpless grief;
He saw, and — O, amazing love! —
    He flew to our relief.

3 Down from the shining seats above
    With joyful haste he fled;
Entered the grave in mortal flesh,
    And dwelt among the dead.

4 O, for this love, let rocks and hills
    Their lasting silence break,
And all harmonious human tongues
    The Saviour's praises speak!

5 Angels, assist our mighty joys;
    Strike all your harps of gold;
But when you raise your highest notes,
    His love can ne'er be told.

142   L. M.

PRAISE God, from whom all blessings flow;
    Praise him, all creatures here below;
Praise him above, ye heavenly host;
Praise Father, Son, and Holy Ghost.

143
P. M.

REMEMBER, sinful youth, you must die,
you must die.
Remember, sinful youth, you must die;
Remember, sinful youth,
Who hate the ways of truth,
And in your folly boast, you must die, you, &c.,
And in your folly boast, you must die.

2 To the great judgment-day, you are bound,
you are bound
To the great judgment-day, you are bound;
To the great judgment-day,
Your thoughts be what they may,
Though you do go astray, you are bound,
you are bound.
Though you do go astray, you are bound.

144
6s. 8s.

REJOICE, the Lord is King;
Your Lord and King adore;
Mortals, give thanks and sing,
And triumph evermore;
Lift up your hearts, lift up your voice;
Rejoice, again I say, rejoice.

2 Jesus, the Saviour, reigns,
The God of truth and love;
When he had purged our stains,
He took his seat above;
Lift up your hearts, lift up your voice;
Rejoice, again I say, rejoice.

3 Rejoice in glorious hope,
Jesus the Judge shall come,

And take his servants up
    To their eternal home;
We soon shall hear th' archangel's voice;
The trump of God shall sound,—Rejoice!

145   L. M.

RETURN, my soul, enjoy thy rest;
  Improve the day thy God hath blest:
Another six days' work is done;
Another Sabbath is begun.

2 O that our thoughts and thanks may rise,
As grateful incense to the skies;
And draw from Christ that sweet repose,
Which none but he that feels it knows.

3 This heavenly calm within the breast,
Is the dear pledge of glorious rest,
Which for the Church of God remains,
The end of cares, the end of pains.

4 In holy duties, let the day,
In holy comforts, pass away;
How sweet, a Sabbath thus to spend,
In hope of one that ne'er shall end.

146   8s. 7s.

RIGHTEOUS God! whose vengeful vials
  All our fears and thoughts exceed,
Big with woes and fiery trials,
  Hanging bursting o'er our head;
While thou visitest the nations
  Thy selected people spare;
Arm our cautioned souls with patience,
  Fill our humbled hearts with prayer.

2 If thy dreadful controversy
   With all flesh is now begun,
In thy wrath remember mercy;
   Mercy first and last be shown.
Plead thy cause with sword and fire;
   Shake us till the curse remove;
Till thou com'st, the saints' desire.
   Crowning them with perfect love.

3 Every fresh alarming token
   More confirms the faithful word;
Nature, for its Lord hath spoken,
   Must be suddenly restored.
From this national confusion,
   From this ruined earth and skies,
See the times of restitution,
   See the new creation rise!

147   7s.

ROCK of ages, cleft for me,
   Let me hide myself in thee;
Let the water and the blood,
From thy side, a healing flood,
Be of sin the double cure,
Save from wrath, and make me pure.

2 Should my tears forever flow,
Should my zeal no languor know,
These for sin could not atone;
Thou must save, and thou alone;
In my hand no price I bring;
Simply to thy cross I cling.

3 While I draw this fleeting breath,
When mine eyelids close in death,
When I rise to worlds unknown,

And behold thee on thy throne,—
Rock of ages, cleft for me,
Let me hide myself in thee.

148   8s. 6s.

SALEM'S great King, Jesus by name,
In ancient time to Jordan came,
  All righteousness to fill;
'Twas there the ancient Baptist stood
Whose name was John, a man of God,
  To do his Master's will.

2 Down in old Jordan's rolling stream,
The Baptist led the holy Lamb,
  And there did him baptize;
Jehovah saw his darling Son,
And was well pleased with what he'd done,
  And owned him from the skies.

3 This is my Son, Jehovah cries;
On him to rest the Spirit flies:
  O children, hear ye him!
Hark! 'tis his voice; behold he cries,
Repent, believe, and be baptized,
  And wash away your sin!

4 Come, children, come; his voice obey:
Salem's bright King has marked the way,
  And has a crown prepared;
O then arise and give consent,
Walk in the way that Jesus went,
  And have the great reward!

149
P. M.

SAW ye my Saviour? saw ye my Saviour?
Saw ye my Saviour and God?
Oh, he died on Calvary,
To atone for you and me,
And to purchase our pardon with blood.

2 He was extended, he was extended,
Painfully nailed to the cross;
There he bowed his head and died,
There my Lord was crucified,
To atone for a world that was lost.

3 Jesus hung bleeding, Jesus hung bleeding,
Three dreadful hours in pain;
And the solid rocks were rent,
Through creation's vast extent,
When the Jews crucified the Lamb.

4 Hail, mighty Saviour! hail, mighty Saviour,
Prince and the Author of peace,
Soon he burst the bands of death,
And triumphant, from the earth,
He ascended to mansions of bliss.

150
C. M.

SALVATION! oh, the joyful sound,
Glad tidings to our ears;
A sovereign balm for every wound,
A cordial for our fears.

2 Salvation! let the echo fly
The spacious earth around;
While all the armies of the sky
Conspire to raise the sound.

3 Salvation! O thou bleeding Lamb,
  To thee the praise belongs:
Salvation shall inspire our hearts,
  And dwell upon our tongues.

151   C. M.

SAY, brothers, will you meet us
  On Canaan's happy shore?
By the grace of God we'll meet you
  Where parting is no more.

2 Jesus lives and reigns forever
  On Canaan's happy shore!
Glory, glory, hallelujah,
  Forever, evermore!

152   C. M.

SEE Israel's gentle Shepherd stands
  With all-engaging charms:
Hark, how he calls the tender lambs,
  And folds them in his arms.

2 Permit them to approach, he cries,
  Nor scorn their humble name;
For 'twas to bless such souls as these
  The Lord of angels came.

3 We bring them, Lord, in thankful hands,
  And yield them up to thee;
Joyful that we ourselves are thine,
  Thine let our offspring be.

153   8s.

SAVIOUR, haste; our souls are waiting
  For the long expected day,
When, new heavens and earth creating,
  Thou shalt banish grief away;
    All the sorrow
Caused by sin and Satan's sway.

2 Haste, O hasten thine appearing!
  Take thy mourning people home;
'Tis this hope our spirits cheering,
  While we in the desert roam,
    Makes thy people
  Strangers here till thou dost come.

3 Lord, how long shall the creation
  Groan and travail, sore in pain;
Waiting for its sure salvation,
  When thou shalt in glory reign,
    And, like Eden,
  This sad earth shall bloom again?

154   L. M.

SHOW pity, Lord, O Lord, forgive;
Let a repenting rebel live.
Art not thy mercies large and free?
May not a sinner trust in thee?

2 My crimes are great, but don't surpass
The power and glory of thy grace;
Great God, thy nature hath no bound,—
So let thy pard'ning love be found.

3 O wash my soul from every sin,
And make my guilty conscience clean;
Here on my heart the burden lies,
And past offences pain my eyes.

4 My lips with shame my sins confess,
Against thy law, against thy grace;
Lord, should thy judgments grow severe,
I am condemn'd, but thou art clear.

5 Yet save a trembling sinner, Lord,
Whose hope, still hov'ring round thy word,
Would light on some sweet promise there;—
Some sure support against despair.

155   P. M.

SINNER, go; will you go
  To the highlands of heaven?
Where the storms never blow,
  And the long summer's given;
Where the bright, blooming flowers
  Are their odors emitting;
And the leaves of the bowers
  In the breezes are flitting.

2 Where the rich golden fruit,
  Is in bright clusters pending,
And the deep-laden boughs
  Of Life's fair tree, are bending.
And where Life's crystal stream,
  Is unceasingly flowing,
And the verdure is green,
  And eternally growing.

3 Where the saints robed in white—
  Cleansed in Life's flowing fountain;
Shining beauteous and bright,
  They inhabit the mountain.
Where no sin nor dismay,
  Neither trouble nor sorrow,
Will be felt for a day,
  Nor be feared for the morrow.

4 He's prepared thee a home—
  Sinner, canst thou believe it?
And invites thee to come,
  Sinner, wilt thou receive it?

Oh come, sinner, come,
  For the tide is receding;
And the Saviour will soon,
  And forever, cease pleading!

156   7s.

SINNERS, turn; why will ye die?
God, your Maker, asks you why?
God, who did your being give,
Made you with himself to live;
He the fatal cause demands;
Asks the work of his own hands,—
Why, ye thankless creatures, why
Will ye cross his love, and die?

2 Sinners, turn; why will ye die?
God, your Saviour, asks you why?
He, who did your souls retrieve,
Died himself, that ye might live.
Will ye let him die in vain?
Crucify your Lord again?
Why, ye ransom'd sinners, why
Will ye slight his grace, and die?

157   7s.

SON of God, thy people's shield,
  Must we still thine absence mourn!
Let thy promise be fulfilled;
  Thou hast said, "I will return."
Gracious Master, soon appear,
  Quickly bring thy morning light;
Then will cease the constant tear,
  Hope be turned to joyful sight.

2 As a woman counts the days
    Till her absent Lord she see,
Longs and watches, weeps and prays,
    So the church must long for thee.
Come, that we may see thee nigh,
    Then the sheep shall feed in peace,
Hush forever trouble's sigh,
    Sin and sorrow's triumph cease.

158 C. M.

SINCE Jesus freely did appear,
    To grace a marriage feast,
O Lord! we ask thy presence here;
    Be thou our glorious guest.

2 Upon thy servants, Lord, look down,
    Who now have joined their hands;
Their union with thy favor crown,
    And bless their nuptial bands.

3 With gifts of grace their hearts endow—
    Of all rich dowries best;
Their substance bless, and peace bestow,
    To sweeten all the rest.

4 In purest love their souls unite,
    That they with Christian care
May make domestic burdens light,
    By taking each a share.

5 True helpers may they prove indeed,
    In prayer, and faith, and hope;
And see with joy a godly seed,
    To build their household up.

6 That love which Jesus Christ displays
    Towards the church, his bride,
Be this, O Lord, through all their days
    Their pattern and their guide.

159
S. M.

SOLDIERS of Christ, arise,
    And put your armour on,
Strong in the strength which God supplies
    Through his eternal Son;
Strong in the Lord of hosts,
    And in his mighty power,
Who in the strength of Jesus trusts,
    Is more than conqueror.

2 Stand then in his great might,
    With all his strength endued;
But take, to arm you for the fight,
    The panoply of God:
That having all things done,
    And all your conflicts past,
Ye may o'ercome, through Christ alone,
    And stand entire at last.

160
L. M.

STAR of our hope. He'll soon appear,
    The last loud trumpet speaks him near;
Hail him all saints, from pole to pole,—
How welcome to the faithful soul!

2 From heaven angelic voices sound,
Behold the Lord of glory crowned,
Arrayed in majesty divine,
And in his highest glory shine.

3 The grave yields up its precious trust,
Which long has slumber'd in the dust;
Resplendent forms ascending fair,
To meet the Saviour in the air.

4 Descending with his azure throne,
He claims the Kingdom for his own;
The saints rejoice, they shout, they sing
And hail him their triumphant King.

161 L. M.

STAY, thou insulted Spirit, stay,
  Though I have done thee such despite;
Nor cast the sinner quite away,
  Nor take thine everlasting flight.

2 Though I have steel'd my stubborn heart,
  And shaken off my guilty fears;
And vex'd, and urged thee to depart,
  For many long rebellious years:

3 Though I have most unfaithful been,
  Of all who e'er thy grace received;
Ten thousand times thy goodness seen;
  Ten thousand times thy goodness grieved:

4 Yet, O! the chief of sinners spare,
  In honor of my great High Priest;
Nor in thy righteous anger swear
  T' exclude me from thy people's rest.

162 L. M.

SWEET is the work, my God, my King,
  To praise thy name, give thanks, and sing;
To show thy love by morning light,
And talk of all thy truth at night.

2 Sweet is the day of sacred rest;
No mortal cares shall fill my breast;
O, may my heart in tune be found,
Like David's harp of solemn sound!

3 My heart shall triumph in the Lord,
And bless his works, and bless his word:
His works of grace, how bright they shine!
How deep his counsels, how divine!

4 And I shall share a glorious part,
When grace hath well refined my heart,
And fresh supplies of joy are shed,
Like holy oil, to cheer my head.

5 Then I shall see, and hear, and know,
All I desired or wished below,
And every power find sweet employ
In that eternal world of joy.

163   C. M.

THAT awful day will surely come,
   Th' appointed hour makes haste,
When I must stand before my Judge,
   And pass the solemn test.

2 Jesus, thou source of all my joys,
   Thou ruler of my heart,
How could I bear to hear thy voice,
   Pronounce the sound, "Depart!"

3 The thunder of that awful word
   Would so torment my ear,
'Twould tear my soul asunder, Lord,
   With most tormenting fear.

4 O wretched state of deep despair,
   To see my God remove,
And fix my doleful station where
   I must not taste his love!

164   C. M.

THE Lord of Sabbath let us praise,
  In concert with the blest,
Who, joyful in harmonious lays,
  Employ an endless rest.

2 Thus, Lord, while we remember thee,
  We blest and pious grow;
By hymns of praise we learn to be
  Triumphant here below.

3 On this glad day a brighter scene
  Of glory was display'd,
By the eternal Word, than when
  This universe was made.

4 He rises, who mankind has bought,
  With grief and pain extreme:
'Twas great to speak the world from naught;
  'Twas greater to redeem.

165   P. M.

THE groaning earth is too dark and drear
  For the saints' eternal home;
But the city from heaven will soon be here;
We know that the moment is drawing near
  When she in her glory shall come.
Her gates of pearl we soon shall see,
  And her music we soon shall hear;
Joyous and bright our home shall be,
And we'll walk in the shadow of life's fair [tree,
  With our Saviour forever near.

2 We'll gladly exchange a world like this,
  Where death triumphant reigns,
For a beautiful home in that land of bliss
Where all is happiness, joy and peace,
  And nothing can enter that pains.

There is no more sorrow and no more night,
  For the darkness shall pass away,
The crucified Lamb is its glorious light,
And the saints shall walk with him in white
  In the happy, endless day.

166 P. M.

THE God of Abrah'm praise,
  Who reigns enthroned above:
Ancient of everlasting days,
  And God of love:
JEHOVAH, GREAT I AM!
  By earth and heaven confess'd;
I bow and bless the sacred Name,
  Forever blest.

2 The God of Abrah'm praise,
  At whose supreme command
From earth I rise, and seek the joys
  At his right hand:
I all on earth forsake,
  Its wisdom, fame, and power;
And him my only portion make,
  My shield and tower.

3 The God of Abrah'm praise,
  Whose all-sufficient grace
Shall guide me all my happy days
  In all his ways:
He calls a worm his friend:
  He calls himself my God!
And he shall save me to the end,
  Through Jesus' blood.

167   P. M.

THE last lovely morning,
  All blooming and fair,
Is fast onward fleeting,
  And soon will appear;

CHORUS.

While the mighty trump sounds,
  "Come, come away!"
O, let us be ready
  To hail the glad day.

2 And when that bright morning
  In splendor shall dawn,
Our tears will be ended,
  Our sorrows all gone;

3 The Bridegroom from glory
  To earth shall descend;
Ten thousand bright angels
  Around him attend;

4 The graves will be opened,
  The dead will arise,
And with the Redeemer
  Mount up to the skies.

168   L. M.

THE morning flowers display their sweets,
  And gay their silken leaves unfold,
As careless of the noontide heats,
  As fearless of the evening cold.

2 Nipt by the winds' untimely blast,
  Parched by the sun's directer ray,
The momentary glories waste,
  The short-lived beauties die away.

3 So blooms the human face divine,
   When youth its pride of beauty shows;
Fairer than spring the colors shine,
   And sweeter than the virgin rose.

4 But worn by slowly rolling years,
   Or broke by sickness in a day,
The fading glory disappears,
   The short-lived beauties die away.

5 Yet these, new rising from the tomb,
   With lustre brighter far shall shine,
Revive with ever-during bloom,
   Safe from diseases and decline.

169   C. M.

THERE is a fountain filled with blood,
   Drawn from Immanuel's veins;
And sinners, plunged beneath that flood,
   Lose all their guilty stains.

2 The dying thief rejoiced to see
   That fountain in his day;
And there may I, though vile as he,
   Wash all my sins away.

3 Dear dying Lamb, thy precious blood
   Shall never lose its power,
Till all the ransomed church of God
   Be saved, to sin no more.

4 Then in a nobler, sweeter song,
   I'll sing thy power to save,
When this poor lisping, stammering tongue
   Is ransomed from the grave.

170   P. M.

THERE is a world to come,
   Happy and pure;
That is the Christian's home,
   Long to endure.
O, 'tis a world of light!
No more death, nor wo, nor night;
Faith views it with delight,
   Knowing 'tis sure.

2 There Christ will ever reign
   All-glorious King!
There music's rapt'rous strain
   Ever will ring;
Saints who in ages by
Suffered, and were called to die,
There in sweet harmony
   Anthems will sing.

3 There is our paradise,
   Eden restored;
All beauteous in their eyes,
   Who love the Lord;
Wastes that are now so drear,
Like the rose shall blossom there,
And be a garden fair:
   Thus saith the word.

171   P. M.

THERE is a happy land,
   Far, far away—
Where saints in glory stand,
   Bright, bright as day.

Oh, how they sweetly sing,
Worthy is our Saviour King;
Loud let his praises ring
   For evermore.

2 Come to this happy land,
   Come, come away;
Why will ye doubting stand?
   Why still delay?
Oh, we shall happy be,
When, from sin and sorrow free,
Lord, we shall live with thee,
   Blest evermore.

3 Bright, in that happy land,
   Beams every eye;
Kept by a Father's hand,
   Love cannot die.
Oh, then to glory run;
Be a crown and kingdom won;
And bright above the sun,
   Reign evermore.

172   P. M.

1 THERE is a land, a better land than this—
   There's my home, there's my home;
A land of pure, unbounded, perfect bliss—
   There's my home, there's my home.
A captive on this desert shore,
I long to count my exile o'er,
And be where sorrows come no more:
   There's my home, there's my home.

2 Far, far I am from my own happy shore—
   I would go, I would go;
But yet my days of exile are not o'er—
   I would go, I would go;

I would not stay though earth were mine;
Though all its treasures for me shine,
A captive here, I still should pine:
　I would go, I would go.

3 Bright visions of that blissful land appear—
　There's my home, there's my home.
How long a pilgrim must I wander here?
　There's my home, there's my home;
O, tell me that I soon shall be
With all the ransomed exiles free
There in that land I long to see!
　There's my home, there's my home.

173　　　　　　　　　　　　C. M.

THIS book is all that's left me now,
　Tears will unbidden start,
With falt'ring heart and throbbing brow,
　I press it to my heart.
My mother's hand this Bible clasped;
　She, dying, gave it me.
For many generations past,
　Here is our family tree.

2 Ah! well do I remember those
　Whose names these records bear;
Who round the hearth-stone used to close,
　After the evening prayer,
And tell of what those pages said,
　In terms my heart would thrill!
Though they are with the silent dead,
　Here are they living still.

3 My father read this holy book
　To brothers, sisters dear;
How calm was my poor mother's look,
　Who loved God's word to hear.

Her angel face,—I see it yet!
   What thronging memories come!
Again that little group is met,
   Within the walls of home.

4 Thou truest friend man ever knew,
   Thy constancy I've tried;
Where all were false I found thee true,
   My counsellor and guide.
The mines of earth no treasures give,
   That could this volume buy;
In teaching me the way to live,
   It taught me how to die.

174   S. M.

THOU Judge of quick and dead,
   Before whose awful bar,
With holy joy or guilty dread,
   We all must soon appear;
Our souls by grace prepare
   For that tremendous day,
And fill us now with watchful care,
   And stir us up to pray.

2 To pray and wait the hour,
   That awful hour unknown,
When, robed in majesty and power,
   Thou shalt from heaven come down;
Th' immortal Son of man,
   To judge the human race,
With all the Father's dazzling train,
   With all thy glorious grace.

175   C. M.

THY life I read, my gracious Lord,
  With transport all divine;
Thine image trace in every word,
  Thy love in every line.

2 Methinks I see a thousand charms
   Spread o'er thy lovely face,
While infants in thy tender arms
   Receive the smiling grace.

3 I take these little lambs, said he,
   And lay them in my breast;
Protection they shall find in me,
   In me be ever blest.

4 His words the happy parents hear,
   And shout, with joys divine,—
O Saviour, all we have and are
   Shall be forever thine.

176   P. M.

TO-DAY the Saviour calls,
  Ye wanderers, come!
O, ye benighted souls,
  Why longer roam?

2 To-day the Saviour calls!
   For refuge fly;
The storm of vengeance falls,
   Ruin is nigh.

3 To-day the Saviour calls!
   O, listen now!
Within these sacred walls
   To Jesus bow.

4 The Spirit calls to-day!
　　Yield to his power;
　O, grieve him not away!
　　'Tis mercy's hour.

177　　　　　　　　　P. M.

'TIS the last call of mercy
　　That lingers for thee;
O, sinner, receive it!
　　To Jesus now flee.
He often has called thee,
　　But thou hast refused;
His offered salvation
　　And love is abused.

2 If thou slightest this warning,
　　Now offered at last,
Thine will be the sad mourning:
　　"The harvest is past,
Salvation I've slighted,
　　The summer is o'er,
And now there is pardon,
　　Sweet pardon, no more."

178　　　　　　　　　7s, 6s.

THE glorious day is coming,
　　The hour is rolling on,
Its radiant light is beaming,
　　Resplendent as the sun;
In yon bright clouds of heaven
　　The Saviour will appear,
And gather all his chosen
　　To meet him in the air.

2 Then fire, from God descending,
   Shall sweep this wide earth o'er,
And nations, loud lamenting,
   Shall sink to rise no more.
Though tears with groans are blended,
   Yet still in vain they cry,
The day of hope is ended:
   The sinner now must die.

3 But saints shall be victorious,
   And joy to meet the Lord;
An earth more bright and glorious
   Is promised in his word.
Our God himself, there reigning,
   Shall wipe all tears away;
No clouds or night remaining,
   But one eternal day.

4 O, Christian, wake from sleeping,
   And let your works abound;
Be watching, praying, weeping,
   For soon the trump will sound!
O, sinner, hear the warning;
   To Jesus quickly fly;
Then you on that blest morning
   May meet him in the sky!

179   7s. 6s.

THE clouds at length are breaking;
   The dawn will soon appear,
And signs there's no mistaking,
   Proclaim Messiah near.
Awake, awake from sleeping,
   Attend the midnight cry;
Ye saints, refrain from weeping,
   Your great Deliv'rer's nigh.

2 The morning light is beaming;
  The day-star shines on high;
Christ's heralds are proclaiming
  His coming in the sky;
And earth's eventful story
  A few short months may tell;
The righteous rise to glory,
  The wicked sink to hell.

3 Great Author of compassion,
  Redeemer, Saviour, Friend,
O, send to every nation
  The knowledge of its end!
Fly, fly on wings of morning,
  Ye who the truth can tell,
And sound the awful warning,
  To rescue souls from hell!

180   P. M.

THE God of harvest praise;
  In loud thanksgiving raise
    Hand, heart, and voice;
The valleys smile and sing,
Forests and mountains ring,
The plains their tribute, bring,
    The streams rejoice.

2 Yea, bless his holy Name,
And purest thanks proclaim
    Through all the earth;
To glory in your lot
Is duty,—but be not
God's benefits forgot,
    Amid your mirth.

3 The God of harvest praise;
Hands, hearts, and voices, raise,
   With sweet accord;
From field to garner throng,
Bearing your sheaves along,
And in your harvest song
   Bless ye the Lord.

181   C. M.

THERE is a land of pure delight,
   Where saints immortal reign;
Infinite day excludes the night,
   And pleasures banish pain.

2 There everlasting spring abides,
   And never-with'ring flowers:
Death, like a narrow sea, divides
   This heavenly land from ours.

3 Sweet fields beyond the swelling flood
   Stand dress'd in living green;
So to the Jews old Canaan stood,
   While Jordan roll'd between.

4 Could we but climb where Moses stood,
   And view the landscape o'er,
Not Jordan's stream, nor death's cold flood,
   Should fright us from the shore.

182   L. M.

THUS far the Lord hath led me on,—
   Thus far his power prolongs my days;
And every evening shall make known
   Some fresh memorial of his grace.

2 Much of my time has run to waste,
   And I, perhaps, am near my home:
But he forgives my follies past,
   And gives me strength for days to come.

3 I lay my body down to sleep;
   Peace is the pillow for my head;
While well-appointed angels keep
   Their watchful stations round my bed.

4 Thus, when the night of death shall come,
   My flesh shall rest beneath the ground,
And wait thy voice to rouse my tomb,
   With sweet salvation in the sound.

183   L. M.

THY kingdom come; thus, day by day,
   We lift our hands to God and pray;
But who has ever duly weighed
The meaning of the words he said?

2 Thy kingdom come; O day of joy,
When praise shall every tongue employ;
When hate, and strife, and war shall cease,
And man with man shall be at peace!

3 Jesus shall reign on Zion's hill,
And all the earth with glory fill;
His word shall Paradise restore,
And sin and death afflict no more.

4 Then bears and wolves, no longer wild,
Obey the leading of a child;
The lions with the oxen eat,
And dust shall be the serpent's meat.

184   P. M.

VAIN, delusive world, adieu,
   With all of creature good;
Only Jesus I pursue,
   Who bought me with his blood.
All thy pleasures I forego,
   I trample on thy wealth and pride;
Only Jesus will I know,
   And Jesus crucified.

2 Other knowledge I disdain;
   'Tis all but vanity;
Christ, the Lamb of God, was slain;
   He tasted death for me.
Me to save from endless wo
   The sin-atoning victim died;
Only Jesus will I know,
   And Jesus crucified.

185   7s.

WAKE the song of Jubilee;
   Let it echo o'er the sea;
Now is come the promised hour;
Jesus reigns with sovereign power.

2 All the nations join and sing,
Praise your Saviour, praise your King,
Let it sound from shore to shore,
"Jesus reigns for evermore!"

3 Hark! the desert lands rejoice;
And the islands join their voice;
Joy! the whole creation sings:
"Jesus is the King of kings!"

186 S. M.

WELCOME, sweet day of rest,
   That saw the Lord arise;
Welcome to this reviving breast,
   And these rejoicing eyes!

2 The King himself comes near,
   And feasts his saints to-day;
Here we may sit, and see him here,
   And love, and praise, and pray.

3 One day in such a place,
   Where thou, my God, art seen,
Is sweeter than ten thousand days
   Of pleasurable sin.

4 My willing soul would stay
   In such a frame as this,
And sit and sing herself away
   To everlasting bliss.

187 C. M.

WITNESS, ye men and angels; now
   Before the Lord we speak;
To him we make a solemn vow,
   A vow we dare not break.

2 That, long as life itself shall last,
   Ourselves to Christ we yield;
Nor from his cause will we depart,
   Or ever quit the field.

3 We trust not in our native strength,
   But on his grace rely,
That, with returning wants, the Lord
   Will all our need supply.

188 P. M.

WEARY pilgrim, why this sadness?
   Why 'mid sorrow's scenes decline?
The "trial strange" brings joy and gladness;
   For all things shall yet be thine;
   O, yes, all things shall yet be thine!

2 Earth anew, with robe of glory,
   Shall rejoice in hill and vale;
And sweetest harpings tell the story
   Of the love that could not fail;
   O, yes, the love that could not fail!

3 Thou shalt range the fields of pleasure,
   Where joy's gushing songs arise;
Thou shalt have all thy well-stored treasure
   In the New Earth, Paradise!
   Yes, in the New Earth, Paradise!

189 S. M.

WE lift our hearts to thee,
   Thou Day-Star from on high!
The sun itself is but thy shade,
   Yet cheers both earth and sky.

2 O, let thy rising beams
   Dispel the shades of night;
And let the glories of thy love
   Come like the morning light!

3 How beaut'ous nature now!
   How dark and sad before!
With joy we view the pleasing change,
   And nature's God adore.

4 May we this life improve
    To mourn for errors past;
And live this short revolving day
    As if it were our last.

190   P. M.

WE'RE travelling home to heaven above,
    Will you go? Will you go?
To sing the Saviour's dying love,
    Will you go? Will you go?
And millions more are on the road,
Millions have reached that blest abode,
Anointed kings and priests to God,
    Will you go? Will you go?

2 We're going to see the bleeding Lamb, &c.
In rapturous strains to praise his name, &c.
The crown of life we there shall wear,
The conqueror's palms our hands shall bear,
And all the joys of heaven we'll share, &c.

3 We're going to join the heavenly choir, &c.
To raise our voice, and tune the lyre, &c.
There saints and angels gladly sing,
Hosanna to their God and King,
And make the heavenly arches ring, &c.

4 Ye weary, heavy-laden, come, &c.
In the blest house there still is room, &c.
The Lord is waiting to receive,
If thou wilt on him now believe,
Thy troubled conscience he'll relieve, &c.

5 The way to heaven is straight and plain, &c.
Repent, believe, be born again, &c.
The Saviour cries aloud to thee,
"Take up thy cross, and follow me,
And thou shalt my salvation see," &c.

191
P. M.

We're going home, we've had visions bright
Of that holy land, that world of light,
Where the long dark night of time is past,
And the morn of eternity's come at last;
Where the weary saint no more shall roam,
But dwell in a sunny, peaceful home;
Where the brow with celestial gems is crowned,
And waves of bliss are dashing round.
  O that beautiful world! O that beautiful world!

2 We're going home, we soon shall be
Where the sky is clear and the soil is free,
Where the victor's song floats o'er the plain,
And the seraph's anthems blend with its strain,
Where the sun rolls down its brilliant flood,
And beams on a world that is fair and good,
And stars, that dimmed at nature's doom,
Will sparkle and dance o'er the new earth's bloom.
  O that beautiful home! O that beautiful home!

3 Where the tears and sighs which here were given
Are exchanged for the gladsome song of heaven,
Where the beauteous forms which sing and shine
Are guarded well by a hand divine.
Pure love's banner and friendship's wand

Are waving above that princely band,
And the glory of God, like a molten sea,
Will bathe that immortal company.
   O that beautiful home! O that beautiful home!

4 Mid the ransomed throng, mid the sea of bliss,
Mid the holy city's gorgeousness,
Mid the verdant plains, mid angels' cheer,
Mid the flowers that never of winter wear;
Where the conqueror's song, as it sounds afar,
Is wafted on the ambrosial air;
Through endless years we then shall prove
The depths of a Saviour's matchless love.
   O that beautiful world! O that beautiful world!

192   P. M.

WE have heard from the bright, the better land;
  We have heard, and our hearts are glad;
For we were a lonely pilgrim band,
  And weary, and worn, and sad.
They tell us the pilgrims ever dwell there,
  No longer are homeless ones;
We know that the goodly land is fair;
  Life's river of water there runs.

2 They say green fields are waving there,
  And they never a blight shall know;
That desert wilds are blooming fair,
  And roses of Sharon grow;
And lovely birds in bowers green
  Their melody ever repeat;
Their warblings mingle, in every scene,
  With harpings of seraphs so sweet.

3 We have heard of the robe, the palm, the
   And the silvery band in white;   [crown,
The city of gems in a high renown,
   Illumined with heavenly light;
The King is seen in his beauty fair,
   The joy and the light of the land;
A little while, and we hope to be there,
   To join with that glorious band.

193   P.M.

WHEN for eternal worlds we steer,
   And seas are calm and skies are clear,
And faith in lively exercise,
And distant hills of Canaan rise:
The soul for joy then claps her wings,
And loud her lovely sonnet sings,
        I'm going home.

2 With cheerful hope her eyes explore,
Each landmark on the distant shore;
The trees of life, the pastures green,
The golden streets, the crystal stream:
Again for joy she claps her wings,
And loud her lovely sonnet sings,
        I'm almost home.

3 The nearer still she draws to land,
More eager all her powers expand;
With steady helm, and full bent sail,
Her anchor drops within the veil;
Again for joy she claps her wings,
And her celestial sonnet sings,
        I'm safe at home.

194
P. M.

WHEN shall we meet again,
  Meet ne'er to sever?
When will peace wreath her chain
  Round us forever?
Our hearts will ne'er repose,
Safe from each blast that blows,
In this dark vale of woes,
  Never, no, never.

2 When shall love freely flow,
  Pure as life's river?
When shall sweet friendship glow
  Changeless forever?
Where joys celestial thrill,
Where bliss each heart shall fill,
And fears of parting chill,
  Never, no, never.

195
L. P. M.

WHO came from Heav'n to ransom me?
  Jesus, who died upon the tree.

CHORUS.
Oh! who's like Jesus? He died on the tree—
He died for you, He died for me;
He died to set poor sinners free:
Oh! who's like Jesus? He died on the tree.

2 Why did He come from heav'n above?
He came because His name was Love.

3 And did He die, the Son of God?
Yes, on the Cross He shed His blood.

4 Why did my Lord and Saviour bleed?
That we from evil might be freed.

5 Christ is the weary sinner's home:
Oh, let us come! Oh, let us come!

195   L. M.

WHEN I survey the wondrous cross,
  On which the Prince of glory died,
My richest gain I count but loss,
  And pour contempt on all my pride.

2 Forbid it, Lord, that I should boast,
  Save in the death of Christ, my God;
All the vain things that charm me most,
  I sacrifice them to thy blood.

3 See from his head, his hands, his feet,
  Sorrow and love flow mingled down!
Did e'er such love and sorrow meet,
  Or thorns compose so rich a crown?

4 Were the whole realm of nature mine,
  That were a present far too small;
Love so amazing, so divine,
  Demands my soul, my life, my all.

196   L. M.

WHEN strangers stand and hear me tell
  What beauties in my Saviour dwell,
Where he is gone they fain would know,
That they may seek and love him too.

2 O may my spirit daily rise
On wings of faith above the skies,
Till I shall make my last remove,
To dwell forever with my love!

3 In paradise, within the gates,
A higher entertainment waits;
Fruits new and old laid up in store;
There we shall feed, but want no more.

197   P. M.

WHO are these in bright array?
  This innumerable throng,
Round the altar night and day
  Tuning their triumphant song?
Worthy is the Lamb once slain,
  Blessing, honor, glory, power,
Wisdom, riches, to obtain:
  New dominion every hour.

2 These through fiery trials trod;
  These from great affliction came;
Now before the throne of God,
  Sealed with his eternal Name:
Clad in raiment pure and white,
  Victor palms in every hand,
Through their great Redeemer's might,
  More than conquerors they stand.

198   P. M.

WHEN the King of kings comes,
  When the Lord of lords comes,
We shall have a joyful day
  When the King of kings comes;
Great Babylon is broken down,
And kingdoms once of great renown,
And saints now suff'ring wear the crown
  When the King of kings comes.

2 When the trump of God calls,
When the last of foes falls,
We shall have a joyful day
  When the King of kings comes;
O then the saints, raised from the dead,
Are with the living gathered,
And all made like their glorious Head,
  When the King of kings comes.

3 When the foe's distress comes,
When the church's "rest" comes;
We shall have a joyful day
   When the King of kings comes:
And then the new Jerusalem,
Surpassing all reports of fame,
Shines, worthy of its Maker's name,
   When the King of kings comes.

199   P. M.

WORTHY, worthy is the Lamb,
   Worthy, worthy is the Lamb,
Worthy, worthy is the Lamb,
   That was slain!
   Glory, hallelujah!
   Praise him, hallelujah!
Glory, hallelujah to the Lamb!

2 Sons of morning, sing his praise
In the noblest strains you raise;
Man's redemption claims your lays;
   Praise the Lamb!
   Glory, hallelujah, &c.

3 Christ has come in very deed,
Born to bruise the serpent's head;
Sing the woman's conq'ring seed;
   Praise the Lamb!
   Glory, hallelujah, &c.

4 See, in sad Gethsemane,
See, on tragic Calvary,
Sinner, see his love to thee;
   Praise the Lamb!
   Glory, hallelujah, &c.

200   H. M.

YE virgin souls, arise;
  With all the dead, awake;
Unto salvation wise,
  Oil in your vessels take:
Upstarting at the midnight cry—
Behold the heavenly Bridegroom nigh!

2 He comes, he comes, to call
  The nations to his bar,
And take to glory all
  Who mete for glory are:
Make ready for your full reward;
Go forth with joy to meet your Lord.

3 Go meet him in the sky,
  Your everlasting Friend;
Your Head to glorify,
  With all his saints ascend:
Ye pure in heart, obtain the grace
To see, without a veil, his face.

4 The everlasting doors
  Shall soon the saints receive,
With seraphs, thrones, and powers,
  In glorious joy to live:
Far from a world of grief and sin,
With God eternally shut in.

201   P. M.

YE who rose to meet the Lord,
  Ventured on his faithful word;
Faint not now, for your reward
  Will be quickly given.

Faint not! always watch and pray;
Jesus will no more delay;
Even now 'tis dawn of day:
    Day-star beams from heaven.

2 Would ye to the end endure?
Keep the wedding garment pure;
Claim ye still the promise sure,
    Faithful is the Lord!
Let your lamps be burning bright;
In God's word is beaming light;
Live by faith, and not by sight;
    Crowns are your reward.

102   L. P. M.

YIELD to me now, for I am weak,
    But confident in self-despair,:
Speak to my heart, in blessings speak;
    Be conquer'd by my instant prayer:
Speak, or thou never hence shalt move,
And tell me if thy name be Love.

2 'Tis Love! 'tis Love! thou diedst for me;
    I hear thy whisper in my heart;
The morning breaks, the shadows flee;
    Pure, universal Love thou art:
To me, to all, thy bowels move,—
Thy nature and thy name is Love.

3 My prayer hath power with God; the grace
    Unspeakable I now receive;
Through faith I see thee face to face;
    I see thee face to face, and live!
In vain I have not wept and strove;
Thy nature and thy name is Love.

CONTENTS.

	PAGE.
Principles of Faith,	6
Basis of Church-Fellowship,	15
Church Order,	15
Marriage Ceremony.	23
Dedication of Children,	25
Baptism.	35
The Lord's Supper,	40
Funeral Service.	33
Ordination of Ruling Elders and Deacons,	46
Ordination of Ministers,	51

HYMNS FOR VARIOUS OCCASIONS.

THE FIGURES REFER TO THE NUMBER OF THE HYMN.

Marriage, 158.
Dedication of Children, 17, 56, 152, 175.
Baptismal Service, 65, 73, 79, 148.
The Lord's Supper, 1, 18, 33, 34, 87.
Funeral Service, 58, 70, 160, 183.
Ordination of Ministers, 54, 94, 103, 110.
Family Devotion, 109, 119, 189.
Covenant with God, 32, 49, 69, 124, 187.
The Sabbath, 145, 162, 164, 186.

www.ingramcontent.com/pod-product-compliance
Lightning Source LLC
Chambersburg PA
CBHW020239170426
43202CB00008B/144